# THE COMMUNION
# OF SAINTS

ALCUIN CLUB COLLECTIONS No. 62

The Alcuin Club exists to promote the study of Christian liturgy in general, and in particular the liturgies of the Anglican Communion. Since its foundation in 1897 it has published over 120 books and pamphlets. Members of the Club receive publications of the current year *gratis*.

Information concerning the annual subscription, applications for membership, and lists of publications is obtainable from the Treasurer, c/o St. Andrew's Vicarage, St. Andrew Street, London EC4 3AB (Telephone 01-353-3544).

# THE COMMUNION OF SAINTS

*An examination of the place of the Christian dead in the belief, worship, and calendars of the Church*

MICHAEL PERHAM

ALCUIN CLUB/S P C K

First published in 1980
for the Alcuin Club
by S P C K
Holy Trinity Church
Marylebone Road
London NW1 4DU


Typeset by CCC, printed and bound in Great Britain by
William Clowes (Beccles) Limited
Beccles and London

ISBN 0 281 03794 9

For Christopher, Dominic,

and Jonathan

# *Contents*

# *Foreword*

It is too much to expect of the very early centuries of Christianity a logical, developed, and unchanging body of doctrine. These were not years of 'orthodoxy' and 'heresy', but of formulation and development. It is particularly unreasonable to expect to find agreement and consistency about questions that involve talk of life after death. At the best of times it is possible to do little more than speculate about them. But for the early Christians changing experience inevitably forced them to rethink their eschatological expectation. The earliest communities of the New Testament expected the end of the world within their own life time and therefore would have wasted little time on the problem of the state of the dead between their death and the end of the world. There was, after all, not very long to wait. So from the very first the idea was present in Christianity that departed souls would not come to enjoy the fellowship of God until the second coming and the last judgement. It was persecution and martydom that first challenged such a view. Was it conceivable that a man who shed his blood for the gospel should be denied an immediate place with his Lord? And so the exceptions began and, though they started with the martyrs, they continued with Old Testament heroes, with ascetics, and with bishops. Into the worlds of the dead came hierarchies and systems about which Christians spoke with increasing confidence and precision, though they were speaking about a highly speculative area of Christian belief.

At times the views they held hardly fitted together into a coherent and logical pattern. But this was in part because heaven and hell, saints and sinners, were not only matters of interest for the theologian, but devotional concerns for the ordinary Christian, for whom theological consistency was never a real issue. The Christian felt instinctively that his saintly bishop, martyred for his faith, was now enjoying the perfect joy of heaven. No theologian would be able to convince him that it was not so. Piety and devotion, not for the last time in the Christian religion, played a vital role in modifying Christian doctrine. The tensions however remained, continued throughout Christian history and are still with us. The language of popular devotion to the saints is in another world from theological discussion of what meaning we can give in the twentieth century to talk of 'the last things'.

The story is therefore a difficult one to tell and the search for a theological rationale for the commemoration of Christian heroes may be a long one. Some may think it an exploration hardly worth beginning. But Tertullian, writing in the third century, recognised that 'the blood of martyrs is the seed of the Church' and it may well be that a rediscovery of the significance of its saints and heroes, men and women of the present century as well as those of the past, can give the Church the renewed vision and courage that the present age demands.

Five considerations in the life of the Church today have encouraged me to try to make an examination of the role of the saints in the life of the Church and to write this book. The first is that nothing comparable has been attempted in the English language since around the turn of the century and, even then, the treatment was narrower and failed to ask a number of fundamental questions. Had the examination of the subject at that time by men like J. P. Kirsch, Darwell Stone, and H. F. Stewart been much more thorough, there would still be a need now for a radical reappraisal in the light of the theological revolution that the twentieth century has witnessed. As it is, while every other doctrine of Christian orthodoxy has been examined, disputed, and restated, belief about life after death has received relatively little attention until very recently, and belief about the place of heroic sanctity in the life of the Church has been almost totally neglected.

In the second place, I have been encouraged to undertake this task simply because of this uncertainty about the 'after life', whatever that may mean. Christian people know that traditional images and pictures are seeming less attractive and credible. Traditional doctrine in terms of heaven, hell, purgatory, and paradise are not preached with much conviction, if at all. Yet concern to know about the life now of those we have known who are now dead, and concern to know also what will happen to us when we die, makes us want to explore the world beyond whatever the uncertainties.

This book has been written with the increasing conviction

that what we say about the great saints of history is, at heart, also what we say about all the departed. The biblical view that sees no real fundamental distinction between 'saints' and all those who have died in Christ's fellowship is a valid one. This is not therefore a book only about figures of giant heroism. It is about Christian sanctity in many forms.

An ecumenical perspective has also influenced the writing of this book. Disagreement about the role of Mary and the saints, and especially about their prayers and about the prayers of the living for the Christian dead, has been a source of friction between Christians of different persuasions. Even if this is no longer the obstacle it was between the theologians of the different churches, it remains a notable difference in the views (or prejudices) of ordinary Christian people. It can be hoped that a book that seeks both to explain how those differences of theology and practice arose, and also in some sense to get behind the 'loaded' theological terms of Reformation and post-Reformation controversies, and to say what we believe about the communion of saints in a new language, may help ecumenical understanding.

A fourth consideration has been the fact that the Church of England is now in the process of reforming its calendar. To watch it doing so has been to witness a very unsatisfactory exercise. There has been, as far as one can detect from the reports of the General Synod and its commissions, an appalling failure to consider fundamental questions about what a saint is, what it means to commemorate a saint, what criteria for sanctity are to be sought, what process is to be required for canonisation or recognition. Provision has already been made for the Alternative Service Book of 1980, but it may not be too late to initiate a discussion that may lead to a more thoughtful approach at any future revision. It is also possible that some of the considerations in this book may be helpful to dioceses and parishes attempting to implement the new proposals in the calendar. For the revision permits a good deal of freedom and choice.

Finally, I have worked with the conviction that, although the Church of the present cannot simply live in the light of the past or even in any sort of imitation of the past, the Church of today can only profit from a rediscovery of the full meaning of belief in 'the communion of saints'. The Church of today should find encouragement in the witness of countless Christians in every age, men and women whose lives give evidence that the Christian God is a God who acts in each generation and is acting still. If the

Church is encouraged and acquires confidence when it thinks of both the witness of the saints down the ages and also the fellowship of all Christian people, living and departed, it also places itself under divine judgement. 'If God was able to do great things in the lives of these faithful ones of the past, how will his Church respond to the divine initiative today?' That is the question with which this book ends. But, in a sense, it is the question that should be asked repeatedly all through the examination of this vast subject.

I have worked with one particular difficulty. The theological confusion of the present day has made it difficult to present a coherent contemporary view of 'the last things'. There has not been the space to examine contemporary views with the care and questioning that I would have liked. If I seem to have accepted a rather easy sort of modification of the traditional views, and to have quoted, with exceptions, only the works of modern Anglican writers, this is not because I am unaware of some deeper and more fundamental questionings about the whole concept of life after death, or of the contributions of writers outside the English and Anglican world. In what is principally a liturgical book, it would have been wrong to spend too much time on speculative theology. But, because I am deeply convinced that good liturgy must grow out of an awareness of theological trends, I have not been afraid to try to show how current theological views, and not only the more extreme or radical ones, challenge some liturgical belief and practice.

I began work on this subject when I was a student at Ripon College, Cuddesdon, Oxford, and I acknowledge the help and interest I received then from staff and students and again when I twice returned in 1978 to continue the work. In particular I place on record my warm thanks to the Reverend Dr. Geoffrey Cuming and the Reverend Brian Smith for their encouragement and advice. I must also thank Mrs. Heather Openshaw, in whose cottage in the Yorkshire Dales I found the peace and quiet to revise and complete the work, and Mr. Timothy Fairbairn for his invaluable help with the proofs and indexes. I owe a great deal to Canon Edward Brooks who, many years ago when he was the parish priest of my childhood days, set me thinking on lines that have led to this book. Neither he nor I, I suspect, know quite how or why he did so, but I am grateful that he did.

MICHAEL PERHAM

Addington 1979

# 1 *The Early Centuries*

## i

The New Testament reveals a tension between two approaches to eschatology—futurist and realised. Because Christian hope is so bound up with the death of Jesus, it has always been important to stress the reality and completeness of present salvation. Yet always there has been a belief that there is more to come—the *parousia*, the resurrection of the dead, the judgement, and the end of the world. The earliest Christians, though they lived with this tension, thought of it as a problem, if they considered it a problem at all, with which they would not have to live for long. They were living, they thought, in the last times. There was no precise theological definition of the relationship between the 'last things' and, at first, no real attempt to define what happened to the Christian dead before the *parousia* and the events that it ushered in.

The view that Christ would come to judge the living and the dead and that a full experience of heaven was not possible for the dead until after that universal judgement outlived the first period of Christian hope when the judgement was thought to be imminent. Even when Christians came to realise that they had been mistaken in expecting a swift end to the world order, they continued to cling to a judgement that would be universal at the end of the world. Even if here and there the idea of individual judgement at the moment of death was creeping in, this was not part of the main stream of eschatological thought. The judgement was to be in the future and it was to be universal. The Son of God would return and separate good from bad. The first-century *Epistle of Barnabas* asserts that

> each will receive according to his deeds. If he be good, his righteousness will go before him; but if he be evil, the recompense of his evil is in store for him.[1]

Hermas, a century later, expected the Son of God to return to earth to separate the good from the bad and to sort out the confusion in which they had lived on earth. The wicked, the impenitent, false teachers, and those who had rejected God would be condemned to destruction and eternal death. But the righteous would dwell with the angels and would have everlasting joy to crown their sufferings and trials. The present world would perish by blood and fire and the whole cosmic order would be transformed.[2]

Hermas probably wrote *c.* 150. From about that date, Christian eschatology entered a new phase of more precise theological definition, chiefly for apologetic reasons in reaction to Judaism and paganism. There was, for instance, a need to resist the Gnostic tendency to dissolve Christian eschatology into the myth of the soul's upward ascent and return to God. Justin taught, on the basis of Old Testament prophecy, not only that Christ would come again in glory, but also that he would come to Jerusalem where he would be recognised by the Jews who dishonoured him and where he would eat and drink with his disciples. Then would begin a reign of a thousand years.[3] This millenarianism came to find increasing support among Christian teachers. Jerusalem would be rebuilt and enlarged. The Christian saints, with the heroes of the Old Testament, would reign there with Christ.

For the great heroes of the faith, therefore, as much as for the ordinary believer, there was to be in the future an event that would transform their existence. They were not already enjoying a life that would have no change or end. What then did happen to the departed soul that awaited the resurrection and the judgement? By the time of Irenaeus, this had become a real question, partly because the Gnostics asserted that the soul passed to heaven immediately after death. Writing towards the end of the second century, Irenaeus draws a parallel with the experience of Jesus who descended to Hades, the place of the dead, for three days. Since no servant is above his master,

> the souls go to an invisible place designated for them by God, and sojourn there until the resurrection. . . . Afterwards, receiving bodies and rising again perfectly, that is with their bodies, just as the Lord himself rose, they will so come to the sight of God.[4]

Tertullian followed a similar line, believing that all souls would remain in the underworld until the day of the Lord, which would not come until the earth had been destroyed, the just being meanwhile consoled with the expectation of the resurrection, and the sinful receiving a foretaste of their future condemnation.[5]

But for both Irenaeus and Tertullian there is a single exception to this picture. The martyrs were considered to be in a special position. What that position was and how it was given a theological rationale will be discussed later.[6] But the existence of an exception inevitably raises the question of whether, in this period of theological development and formulation, there were other exceptions or even other views of after life. What, for instance, can be made of these words from the *Odes of Solomon*?

> Death has been destroyed before my face,
> and Sheol has been vanquished by my word.
> And eternal life has arisen in the Lord's land,
> and it has been declared to his faithful ones,
> and been given without limit to all that trust in him.[7]

Scholars are divided about the source of the *Odes of Solomon*, but they certainly belong to the first or second century and are now generally accepted to be Christian. They speak of 'eternal life' in something of the same way as John's gospel, but they apply it far more explicitly to a life after earthly life. They imply a life in which the souls of the righteous have been freed from Hades by Jesus and now are free with him in heaven. There is no reference to martyrdom. Those who are free are not those who have earned their release, but those who

> cried out and said, 'Son of God, have pity on us. And deal with us according to thy kindness, and bring us out from the bonds of darkness and open for us the door by which we may come out to thee, for we perceive that our death does not touch thee.'[8]

It is quite a different eschatological view point from that of Hermas, Justin, and Irenaeus. Whether it is representative of any main stream Christian thinking of the time is doubtful. Clearly it is very much under Gnostic influence, though its Christological language is far closer to the fathers than most Gnostic literature. But its existence, even among a fringe group, suggests a very early date for a theological view of after life that categorized men and women into those who at death went to be with God and those for whom a period of waiting and cleansing was required.

ii

Christian eschatology developed against a background of persecution. The fact that Irenaeus and Tertullian both made exceptions of the martyrs in presenting their view of after life demonstrates how the increasing experience of punishment and death within the Christian communities modified outlooks. The Roman government was by no means always intolerant of foreign religions. National religions were respected and indeed for a time Christianity was able to shelter under the cloak of Judaism, itself a national religion allowed to pursue its own course. Christians, however, became controversial and were thought dangerous quite early on. Their loyalty was suspected because they refused to worship the emperor. Their numbers posed a threat. Their supposed customs, principally accusations of cannibalism arising from a misunderstanding of eucharistic language, aroused scandal. Until *c.* 250 the extent of persecution by the state was determined more by local feeling than by imperial policy. But from the very first Christianity had its martyrs. The death of Stephen and of James is recorded in the Acts of the Apostles. Nero used Christians as scapegoats for the fire of Rome in A.D.64. Though his victims were condemned for arson rather than for holding a particular belief, a precedent was set for treating Christians generally as criminals, and condemning them 'for the Name' by summary magisterial jurisdiction. Polycarp died at Smyrna in 156 and Justin at Rome a few years later under Marcus Aurelius. These were not isolated incidents, but the real period of systematic persecution began under the emperor Decius in 250. He ordered all subjects to sacrifice to the state gods under pain of death. Led by men like Cyprian, the Church resisted. Valerian, who succeeded Decius, continued the same policy of repression, arresting bishops and executing all the clergy and laymen of high rank who would not renounce their faith. After his death the Church was given a brief respite before Diocletian's persecution, begun in 304, brought the Church its greatest testing. It survived. The very ferocity and intensity of the attack won support for the Church from people sickened by the cruelty. Bloodshed failed to achieve its purpose and the worst period of persecution led swiftly to the edicts of toleration at the beginning of the fourth century.

Some of the early martyrdoms are very well documented. One Christian community sent to another accounts of the trials and persecutions which its leaders endured. The Christians in Smyrna, for instance, sent a letter to 'the church of God which dwells in Philomelium and to all the dioceses of the holy catholic Church in every place', the purpose of which was to tell

> the story of the martyrs and of blessed Polycarp, who put an end to the persecution, setting his seal thereto by his martyrdom. For almost all that went before so happened, that the Lord might shew forth anew an example of martyrdom which is conformable to the gospel.[9]

The record that follows of the martyrdom of Polycarp is the first authentic narrative of a Christian martyrdom after those of the New Testament.

Polycarp was betrayed by a servant and arrested one evening at a farm outside Smyrna. He was brought into the city and to the stadium where the proconsul tried to persuade him to deny his faith. '"Curse Christ!" Polycarp answered, "Eighty and six years have I served him, and he did me no wrong. How can I blaspheme my king, that saved me?"'[10] Repeated attempts by the proconsul to persuade him to renounce his faith proved fruitless. Polycarp, full of confidence and joy, could not be persuaded and so he was ordered to be burnt alive, the people meanwhile yelling for his blood. The contemporary account continues:

> He, with his hands bound behind him, like a choice ram taken from a great flock for sacrifice, an acceptable whole burnt-offering prepared for God, looked up to heaven and said: 'Lord God Almighty, Father of thy well-beloved and blessed Son, Jesus Christ, through whom we have received the knowledge of thee, God of angels and powers and of the whole creation and of all the race of the righteous who live before thee, I bless thee that thou didst deem me worthy of this day and hour, that I should take a part among the number of the martyrs. . . .' When he had offered up the Amen, and finished his prayer, those who had charge of the fire set light to it. And a great flame blazing forth, we to whom it was given to behold, who were indeed preserved to tell the story to the rest, beheld a marvel. For the fire forming a sort of arch made a wall about the body of the martyr, which was in the midst, not like burning flesh, but like bread in the baking, or like gold and silver burning in a furnace. For we caught a most sweet perfume, like the breath of frankincense or some other precious spice. At last when the impious people saw that his body could not be consumed by the fire they gave orders that a slaughterer should go and thrust a dagger into him.[11]

The church at Smyrna goes on to record how the body was entirely burnt and the bones, 'being of more value than precious stones and more esteemed than gold', retrieved by the Christians and buried. There is about the story very little sadness and fear. The little church over which Polycarp had presided sounded confident and joyful. Not only had Polycarp been a famous teacher, but he had also become an illustrious martyr, whose martyrdom they all wanted to imitate because that was the pattern that the gospel of Christ required of them.

Polycarp's martyrdom has about it the special quality of the death of one who was not only the acknowledged and much loved leader of a Christian community, but also a link with the apostles. For Irenaeus tells us that Polycarp 'had been trained by the apostles and had conversed with many who had seen Christ'.[12] Thus, as the last representative of those who had known the apostles and 'of those who had seen the Lord', he was held in the greatest reverence throughout the Christian world. Despite this, Polycarp's martyrdom is not untypical of the death of Christian believers in many cities in the early centuries of Christianity. About nearly all of them there is the same willingness to suffer and joy in suffering, but among the authentic martyrs this never becomes a search for martyrdom. There is the same refusal to compromise and the same confession of faith. And there is too in every such account a similar devotion among those left behind to the memory of the martyr who is regarded always as a hero, a victor, and an encouragement to those facing similar trials.

One further example must suffice. It is the record of the martyrdom in 203 of Saint Perpetua and her companions which, with its peculiar beauty, has a place of its own among the early martyrdoms. It is perhaps the most moving and impressive of the authentic narratives of the age. The document was written in part by Perpetua herself, in part by another of the martyrs, Saturus, and completed by a third author after the martyrdom. Perpetua was a young married woman of good family with a babe in arms. Her companions included Felicity, a slave girl far advanced in pregnancy. At the time of their arrest at Carthage under an edict of Septimus Severus all of them except Saturus were still catechumens. They were baptised while under house arrest and soon after imprisoned. Perpetua herself takes up the story:

> After a few days a rumour ran that we were to be examined. Moreover, my father arrived from the city, worn with trouble, and came up to see me, that he might overthrow my resolution. . . . And I grieved for my father's sake, because he alone of all my kindred would not have joy in my suffering. And I comforted him, saying: 'It shall happen on that platform as God shall choose; for know well

that we lie not in our own power but in the power of God.' And full of sorrow he left me.[13]

The account of the martyrdom is remarkable not only for this description in the first person of the trials and strains of imprisonment and persecution, but also for the visions which Perpetua and Saturus both had in prison and told to each other and which no doubt sustained them as they faced their ordeal. Saturus records in his vision the arrival of the martyrs in heaven:

> We came near to a place whose walls were built like as it might be of light, and before the gate of that place were four angels standing, who as we entered clothed us in white robes. And we entered, and heard a sound as of one voice saying, 'Holy, holy, holy' without ceasing. And we saw sitting in the same place one like unto a man white-haired, having hair as white as snow, and with the face of a youth; whose feet we saw not. And on the right hand and on the left four elders; and behind them were many other elders standing. And entering we stood in wonder before the throne; and the four angels lifted us up, and we kissed him, and he stroked our face with his hand. And the other elders said to us, 'Let us stand.' And we stood and gave the kiss of peace. And the elders said to us, 'Go and play.' And I said to Perpetua, 'You have your wish.' And she said to me, 'Thanks be to God, that as I was merry in the flesh, so am I now still merrier here.'[14]

Before their martyrdom, Felicity gave birth to a daughter who was at once adopted by a fellow Christian. On the day of their triumph, the martyrs entered the arena, Perpetua coming last, 'the true bride of Christ and darling of God, her piercing gaze abashing all eyes'. A detailed account is given of how Perpetua and Felicity helped each other when attacked by a wild cow, and of the attack on the others by a leopard, bear, and boar.

> And when the people asked for them to be brought into the open, that, when the sword pierced their bodies, these might lend their eyes for partners in the murder, they rose unbidden and made their way whither the people willed, after first kissing one another, that they might perfect their martyrdom with the rite of the *Pax*. The rest without a movement in silence received the sword . . . Perpetua, however, that she might taste something of the pain, was struck on the bone and cried out, and herself guided to her throat the wavering hand of the young untried gladiator. Perhaps so great a woman, who was feared by the unclean spirit, could not otherwise be slain except she willed.[15]

## iii

The Christians of Carthage when they thought about Perpetua and her companions and the Christians of Smyrna when they remembered Polycarp were thankful for the life and death of their hero and were strengthened and encouraged by this memory. But inevitably they found themselves asking 'What has happened to our hero now?' If one had seen Perpetua or Polycarp die for the faith, loyal and steadfast to the last, one would feel instinctively that they would be rewarded by being with God in heaven straight away. 'Having vanquished by his patience the unjust ruler, and thus received the crown of immortality,' writes the church of Smyrna about Bishop Polycarp, 'he rejoices greatly with the apostles and with all the just, and glorifies the almighty God and Father.'[16] But whether Polycarp glorifies God in heaven or whether from an intermediate state where all souls, however virtuous, remain until the final judgement is not entirely clear. Polycarp himself had had no doubt. He had written some years before that he was sure that those who had died for the faith 'ran not in vain, but in faith and justice, and that they are in their due place in the presence of the Lord, with whom also they suffered.'[17] Polycarp was expressing a belief, which we have already noted is found in Irenaeus and Tertullian, that there was a great exception, that of the martyrs, to the belief that the full joys of heaven were not yet for even the most virtuous of the dead. Some of the writers of the time recognised that this introduced an inconsistency into their thinking. If the martyrs were excepted, why not other categories? Attempts to resolve this problem were made. Although all were agreed that the martyrs attained at once to God in heaven, some, like Clement of Alexandria, happily pointed to the door of violent death as being the entrance to true life,[18] while others held the opinion that perfect blessedness would be granted to the martyrs, as to all the other elect including the apostles, only after the end of the world and the final judgement, the martyrs meanwhile enjoying a slightly unsatisfactory, but nevertheless heavenly, existence. Origen, in the third century, believed that all souls must pass throught the fires of purgatory at their entry into the other world, and that those who are stained with sin, although they are destined for paradise, will be purified in the fire. Nevertheless he adds that, when souls arrive in the other world already free from sin, they pass unscathed through this cleansing to their appointed place above the heavens by God's throne.[19]

Christian theologians came to believe that the only way in which the soul could indeed arrive in the other world free from sin was by martyrdom. Martyrdom came to be thought of as a cleansing fire in itself. It was a second baptism, a baptism by fire or a baptism by blood. Origen exhorts his readers in a work on martyrdom, whenever they are in danger of dying a natural death, to consider with him that perhaps they are saved from that sort of death in order that they may be given a place in heaven along with the martyrs.[20] Tertullian talks of martyrdom as 'the second immersion' and 'the second bath'. In an anonymous document, the *Passion of Donatianus and Rogatianus,* Donatianus asks that God will regard the sincere faith of the unbaptised Rogatianus as baptism and the shedding of his blood as confirmation.

If martyrdom served the same purpose as baptism in cleansing from sin and the martyr was therefore guaranteed to arrive in the next world purified, martyrdom became a desirable thing. Indeed in later centuries the formal process of canonisation began to develop in part to prevent those who had foolishly gone out of their way to seek martyrdom from being venerated as martyrs. It was considered wrong to seek martyrdom, but it was quite a worthy thing to desire it. Ignatius, in the very first century of Christianity, wrote to the church at Rome:

> I exhort you, be ye not an unseasonable kindness to me. Let me be given to the wild beasts, for through them I can attain unto God. I am God's wheat, and I am ground by the teeth of wild beasts, that I may be found pure bread of Christ.[21]

Tertullian also believed that martyrdom put a man in a class of his own.

> The Christian is snatched by faith from the jaws of the devil, but by martyrdom he fells to the ground the enemy of his salvation. By faith the Christian is delivered from the devil, by martyrdom he merits the crown of perfect glory over him.[22]

This view of victory over evil is developed further in the Church so that the death of martyrs is seen not only as an encouragement to the faithful but also as a real defeat of evil in such a way that not only the martyr but also others who seek his assistance are cleansed. Imprisoned Christians, who were to die, were asked especially to pray for others. Their prayer together with their death was believed to be particularly acceptable to God. John Chrysostom, in the fourth century, can therefore speak of the death of martyrs as not only 'the exhortation of the faithful' and 'the confidence of the Church', but also as 'the disgrace of devils, denunciation of Satan' and 'the spring, root, and origin of all benefits.'[23] This last phrase marks a significant development in belief about the effectiveness and power of the death of martyrs.

Because of the view that martyrdom was an equivalent of baptism, it was logical to make exceptions of the martyrs and to believe them to be in heaven. But once one set of exceptions had been introduced, there was of course pressure for other groups with special claims. Notable among these were the heroes of the Old Testament and the apostles. In succession to the Old Testament patriarchs and prophets, the apostles followed as the divinely laid foundation of the Church. Hermas, writing in the second century, asserted that after death the apostles and teachers, after falling asleep in the power and faith of the Son of God, preached to the departed saints of the Old Testament and gave them the seal of the preaching. By their efforts the Old Testament heroes were brought to life and came to know the name of the Son of God.[24] Hermas, who in many ways is not typical, clearly regards the apostles and their fellow workers as inheritors already of the joys of heaven. They are in a position of privilege by which they can go to the rescue of the Old Testament figures trapped in the past. Hermas sees the martyrs together with the Old Testament saints and the apostles in heaven.[25] Another early tradition understood the appearance of the saints on the day of the crucifixion as the release of the souls of the patriarchs and prophets.

> There was an earthquake, the rocks split and the graves opened, and many of God's saints were raised from sleep; and coming out of the graves after his resurrection they entered the holy city.[26]

Another tradition, recognising that maryrdom was the key to heaven, assumed that all the apostles were martyrs, for it would be inconceivable that the apostles could remain in the place of the departed while the martyrs enjoyed the life of heaven. But still there were those who were willing to deny the apostles automatic right to be in heaven. Origen, not always consistent, was sometimes among them. He wrote that he believed that the just, the apostles included, did not enjoy the perfect bliss of heaven, for perfect blessedness would only begin after the full number of the elect had been made up.[27]

It was a confused situation in which there were undoubtedly inconsistencies and illogicalities. But all the time there was developing a far wider doctrine that finally found a place in the creeds of the Church, the belief in the 'communion of saints'. The tendency to categorize, to decide the fate of every individual group, whether apostles, martyrs, or whatever, is matched by a tremendous sense of belonging to a fellowship in which the distinctions between saint in heaven, departed Christian in the place of the dead, and living Christian on earth were not only blurred but also unimportant. The danger of grading the departed into those who were in heaven (and for whom it was therefore improper to pray) and those who were in the place of the dead (and for whom it was therefore right to pray) was beginning to take hold of the Church. But at this time the main stream theological view was to emphasise the unity of all the faithful, living and departed, in a unity in which mutual prayer had its place.

## iv

The doctrine of the saints was therefore a part of the doctrine of the Church. There was a sense of belonging to each other, whether in this world or another, that subsequent generations have lost. It was easier for the Christians of Rome, Carthage, and Smyrna to feel close to the Christian martyrs, for those who had died were those whom they had known and honoured and loved in this life. The communion of saints meant fellowship not with distant figures of previous centuries and cultures but with contemporaries who had died for the faith and in the faith. Such was the view that caused the Christians of Smyrna to inform the churches to whom they were writing about the martyrdom of Polycarp that

> we later took up his bones, being of more value than precious stones and more esteemed than gold, and laid them apart in a convenient place. There the Lord will grant us to gather so far as may be and to celebrate with great gladness and joy the birthday of his martyrdom.[28]

When Christians gathered at Polycarp's grave in the years that followed, no doubt they sought the prayers of the martyr for themselves and for others, as Christians did at the graves of all the martyrs. Not only did they gather at the grave, but they buried their departed relatives and friends there in order that they should be reminded to invoke the martyrs in their prayers on behalf of the departed souls. The martyrs came to be regarded as the patrons of the departed buried near them. Their physical proximity led to a hope that the martyrs would take a special interest in them.[29]

But, at this early stage in the development of a doctrine of the saints, prayer was a mutual exercise. The departed were believed to be praying for the living (and could be asked to do so) and the living prayed for the departed, though from a very early date it was felt that the martyrs did not need the prayers of the Christian living because of their unique status in the future life. Perpetua, in prison before her martyrdom prays for her long-dead baby brother:

> While we were all praying, suddenly in the middle of the prayer I spoke, and uttered the name of Dinocrates; and I was astonished that he had never come into mind till then; and I grieved thinking of what had befallen him. And I saw at once that I was entitled, and ought, to make request for him . . . There was besides in the very place where Dinocrates was a font full of water, the rim of which was above the head of the child; and Dinocrates stood on tiptoe to drink. I grieved that the font should have water in it and that nevertheless he could not drink because of the height of the rim. And I awoke and recognised that my brother was in trouble. But I trusted that I could relieve his trouble, and I prayed for him every day.

Perpetua's prayer did not go unanswered. Some time later, in another vision, she saw Dinocrates again in the same place, but now the font which she had seen before had its rim lowered to the child's waist.

> Dinocrates came forward and began to drink from it, and the bowl failed not. And when he had drunk enough of the water, he came forward being glad to play as children will. And I awoke. Then I knew that he had been released from punishment.[30]

This sort of prayer, by the living for the dead, developed throughout the early period. Tertullian writes of a widow who prays for the soul of her departed husband seeking refreshment and a place in the first resurrection for him. Tertullian regards such a practice as one of those things which, though not mentioned in scripture, is universally observed in the Church.[31] Cyprian writes of naming the departed at the Eucharist,[32] and the practice was a constant and regular feature of the liturgy from at least the fourth century onwards. But, as soon as martyrs were put in a category all their own on a different level from the other Christian dead, the idea, inherent in the doctrine of the communion of saints, of the mutual and reciprocal nature of prayer between the living and the dead began to fade, as prayer by the living for the departed was seen as prayer for the souls in Hades, while prayer by the departed for the living was seen as the prayer of the glorified ones in heaven. The saints, regarded as the perfectly holy followers of Christ during their life time and the inheritors of a special place in the heavenly city, were Christ's friends in a higher sense than the rest of the elect. As such, they were regarded as patrons and mediators before God and Christ on behalf of the other members of the Church and could obtain grace and help by their prayer for the faithful, both living and dead. Though the saints were held up as examples to the faithful by the teachers of the church and the imitation of the virtues they had displayed in their life and death was an incentive to perfect Christian living, they were important above all else not as examples but as intercessors able to procure spiritual aids and graces and to give protection and deliverance. Such devotion naturally manifested itself both in the private religious practices of the individual Christian and in the official liturgical ceremonies of the community.

Origen is the first writer to speak of the invocation of saints. He says of 'supplications', 'intercessions' and 'giving of thanks':

> It is not improper to address these to saints, and two of them, I mean intercession and thanksgiving, not only to saints but also to men, but supplication only to saints, as for instance to some Paul or Peter, that they may aid us, making us worthy to obtain the power granted unto them for the forgiveness of sins.[33]

But the evidence for the invocation of saints is scanty until about a hundred years later when it is to be found in the writings of Hilary, Basil, Gregory of Nazianzus, and Gregory of Nyssa.[34] Basil is in no doubt about what sort of prayer is legitimate.

> I accept also the holy apostles, prophets, and martyrs, and I call upon them for their intercession to God, that by them, that is by their mediation, the good God may be propitious to me and that I may be granted redemption for my offences.[35]

Ephraem the Syrian, a friend of Basil who, when Basil died, sought his intercession, also asks the martyrs to be 'intercessors before the throne for me who am vain, that I may be found there, being saved by the help of your intercessions through the grace of our Lord and Saviour Jesus Christ.' At this time there was already emerging a division about the sort of prayer that it was legitimate to make to the saints. Both Basil and Ephraem in these passages are clear that the saints are asked to present prayers to God. The saints are to be intercessors. But Gregory of Nazianzus, in praying to Cyprian, addresses him as if he has power not only to intercede to God but to grant favours in his own right. He asks Cyprian to 'look down on us propitiously from above and direct our speech and life.'[36] At the time that he was writing, Gregory would seem to have been in a minority in regarding the saints as more than intercessors, but, in the centuries that were to follow, his attitude gained wide acceptance.

The prayers to the saints offered by men like Gregory, Basil, and Ephraem were private devotions. But the public commemoration of the saints in the liturgy of the Church also belongs to this period. The gathering at the martyr's tomb on the anniversary of his death was normally for a celebration of the Eucharist. Eusebius (in the first half of the fourth century) asserts that the manner of honouring the martyrs was in the use of their tombs as altars upon which the Eucharist was offered.[37] There was good theological reason for associating the Eucharist and the saints, for the Eucharist was an expression of the Church's unity. The Body of Christ was not simply the Church on earth, but the whole communion of saints. John Chrysostom regarded it as a mark of recognition of the status of martyrs that they should be named in the Lord's presence while his death was being celebrated.[38]

The liturgical commemoration of a saint on the day of his death was the beginning of a calendar. A city would observe on different dates the anniversaries of all its martyrs by a Eucharist celebrated at the tomb, at first in the open air but soon in churches built over the grave. Such calendars would at first have included therefore only the names of local martyrs whose tombs were within or near the city. Gradually, of course, other saints, whose fame had spread, would be commemorated in other cities. It is more than likely that, when the Christians in Smyrna wrote to 'the church of God which dwells in Philomelium and to all the dioceses of the holy catholic Church in every place' about the martyrdom of Polycarp, some of the recipients of that letter began to commemorate Polycarp on the anniversary of his death despite the absence of his tomb from their city. But, at least in Rome, where Polycarp's name did not find its way into the calendar, as far as it is possible to know what it was in its original form, nearly every saint in the calendar was a local hero, martyred in Rome and during a relatively short period of time, in the latter half of the third century and the opening years of the fourth century. To describe Rome as typical is always dangerous, but it is reasonable to suppose that the development of a calendar in Rome was not unlike its development elsewhere, and Rome is the best documented example to take. The Roman calendar lies at the root of the development of the calendar in almost all the historic churches of the west. Though many of the names in it mean little or nothing to us today—what, for instance, do we know about Saint Praxedis?—names like Fabian, Agatha, Lawrence, and Cyprian are still to be found in calendars in use today.

## V

In piecing together the information available in order to reconstruct the first Roman calendar we can build up a comparatively full picture of the liturgical commemoration of the saints in Rome during the fifth, sixth, and seventh centuries, when the persecutions were ending and had ended but while they were still sufficiently close to evoke an emotional response. The work of reconstruction was done half a century ago by Bishop Frere of Truro.[39] Making use of a number of sources, he showed that the saints in the earliest Roman calendar were, with only a few exceptions, of three categories. The first, and probably the normal, way that a saint found his way into the calendar was if the existence of his tomb in or near the city demanded a Eucharist there on the anniversary of his death. Such a Eucharist would have been the Eucharist of the day for the whole city. On 14 October, for instance, we should not imagine a Eucharist in honour of Saint Callistus, an early third-century pope and martyr, being said by each parish priest in his church, but one Eucharist for the whole of Rome celebrated in his honour in the cemetery of the *Via Appia* where he was buried. The churches of martyrs such as Callistus lay at various distances from the city. Most of the big cemeteries lay within a radius of not more than three or four miles from the middle of the city, not an unreasonable distance for Christians to walk to honour the martyrs on their anniversaries. Not only Callistus, but Fabian, Lawrence, Agnes, and many others to be found in the Roman calendar were buried in cemeteries within reasonable distance of the city. But some more distant shrines also received a visit. A journey of fifteen miles was required in order to celebrate the day of Primus and Felician. It was not surprising therefore that in 642 Pope Theodore I had their relics transferred and reburied in the church of Saint Stephen in the city.

A second group of saints found their way into the calendar because there were churches in their honour in the city itself. These were the *tituli* (of which there were twenty-five or, according to some calculations, twenty-two) which were the parish churches of Rome. Originally these churches were known by names that were not necessarily those of saints. One, for instance, was called *titulus Pudentis* because Pudens was the founder of it. In time, however, when the cult of the saints had taken a firmer grip, the same church was said to be dedicated in honour of Saint Pudentiana, who never existed, the name being simply a corruption of the name of the founder. Others, such as *titulus Clementis,* were genuinely named after real saints. Clement had been a first-century bishop of Rome.

In other cases, when a saint was adopted as patron of a church, one was chosen through similarity of the name to that of the founder. This was probably the case with the *titulus Chrysogoni,* for which it was necessary to go as far afield as Aquileia in northern Italy in order to find a saint of the same name. The *tituli* therefore became churches named after a saint. Generally they did contain the burial place of the saint after whom they were named, but it was not long before liturgical commemoration was established around relics. When a church did not contain the tomb of its patron, it sought a relic of him. Soon rather the reverse became the custom, and a church was named after the saint whose relic had been obtained for it at the time of its consecration. The necessity to obtain relics to place in the altar of churches where there was no tomb of a martyr promoted the cult of the martyrs, and such theologians as Hilary, John Chrysostom, Basil, and the two Gregorys sanctioned such veneration.[40] By this means, not only in Rome but throughout the Christian world, the feasts of celebrated martyrs, which had originally been local observances, spread to other localities where some relic of the martyrs was preserved in the churches. The *tituli* therefore soon required a special day to venerate their saint, the Eucharist being celebrated at the altar in which was lodged a relic of the patron saint, instead of an altar that was itself a martyr's tomb. An additional reason for the importance of the *tituli* in the development of the calendar was their use as 'stational churches', in which the 'papal stations' took place. These were the solemn services held at different churches when the pope presided, supported by the twenty-five parish priests and their people. Nearly all the *tituli* were used for these stations and so were the great basilicas of Rome. Inevitably the list of stational churches had a bearing on the development of the calendar, because it was natural that the patron saints to whom these great churches were dedicated should have commemorations assigned to them in the church year.

There is a third group who were commemorated because it was universally thought desirable to honour great heroes of the Christian faith with no local connection. But such observance was very rare, was chiefly of biblical figures and, even among these, concentrated on the New Testament figures whose martyrdom was recorded in scripture. Thus Saint Stephen, the first martyr, is commemorated, though in a rather confused way he is remembered on 2 August, which really belongs to Pope Stephen who was martyred on that day in 255. John the Baptist, whose death is also precisely recorded in the New Testament, also merits a day. Perpetua and Felicity, representative of Africa, also find their way into the Philocalian list, a document dating from the first half of the fourth century, which included memorial days for the martyrs. Yet their commemoration failed to secure a place in the liturgical calendar, presumably because there was neither tomb nor relic in Rome. The lack of real regard for Perpetua and Felicity typifies the lack of interest in any saint for whom there was no church that demanded an anniversary service. The calendar was at first a document that indicated *where* the Eucharist should be celebrated. Only later did it become a directory, not of where the Eucharist was to be offered, but of in whose honour it was to be said by the parish priest in his own church. There is insufficient evidence by which a date could be given for this development. Clearly it was only by stages that the official Eucharist at the cemetery was given up, as the Roman church became simply too big to operate in this way. But the real blow came with the destruction of the catacombs and cemeteries with the fall of Rome. It is impossible to draw up the earliest Roman calendar with any degree of certainty. Bishop Frere, using the Philocalian lists telling what names were honoured in the middle of the fourth century, the Roman martyrology formulated half a century later, the lists of churches, the service books, and the *Liber Pontificalis* (of which the earliest extant copy is in a sixth-century second edition), attempted a tentative reconstruction of the earliest Roman calendar, including only those entries that by common agreement of the different sources belong there. The list of saints in this calendar[41] is a short one:

| *Date* | *Name* | *Date* | *Description* | *Place* | *Notes* |
|---|---|---|---|---|---|
| 14 Jan | Felix | *c.* 260 | no evidence of martyrdom | Nola | |
| 16 | Marcellus | *c.* 309 | pope, not martyr | Rome | D |
| 20 | Fabian | 250 | pope and martyr | Rome | T |
| | Sebastian | ? | martyr | Rome | T |
| 21, 28 | Agnes | *c.* 304 | martyr | Rome | CT |
| 5 Feb. | Agatha | 3rd cent. | martyr | Sicily | CDT |
| 14 | Valentine | ? | martyr | ? | |
| 14 Apr | Tiburtius,[42] Valerian, and Maximus | ? | martyrs | Rome | |
| 28 | Vitalis | ? | martyr | Rome | D |
| 1 May | Philip and James | 1st cent. | apostles and martyrs | (biblical) | CT |
| 12 | Nereus and Achilleus | ? | martyrs | Rome | T |
| | Pancras | 304? | martyr | Rome | T |
| 2 Jun | Peter and Marcellinus | *c.* 304 | martyrs | Rome | CDT |
| 18 | Mark and Marcellian | ? | martyrs | Rome | |
| 19 | Gervasius and Protasius | ? | martyrs | Milan | D |
| 23, 24 | John the Baptist | 1st cent. | martyr | (biblical) | CT |
| 26 | John and Paul | ? | martyrs | ? | CD |
| 28, 29, 30, 6 July | Peter and Paul | 1st cent. | apostles and martyrs | (biblical) Rome | CDT |
| 10 | The Seven Brothers | ? | martyrs | Rome | C[43] |
| 21 | Praxedis | ? | ? | ? | D |
| 30 | Abdon and Sennen | ? | martyrs | Rome | |
| 2 Aug | Stephen[44] | 1st cent. | protomartyr | (biblical) | CDT |
| | | 255 | pope and martyr | Rome | |

| *Date* | *Name* | *Date* | *Description* | *Place* | *Notes* |
|---|---|---|---|---|---|
| 6 Aug | Sixtus, Felicissimus, and Agapitus | 258 | martyrs | Rome | DT |
| 8 | Cyriacus | ? | martyr | Rome | D |
| 9, 10, 17 | Lawrence | 258 | martyr | Rome | CDT |
| 11 | Tiburtius | ? | martyr | Rome | |
| | Susanna | ? | martyr | Rome | D |
| 13 | Hippolytus | *c.* 235 | martyr | Rome | C |
| 18 | Agapitus | ? | martyr | Palestrina | |
| 28 | Hermes | ? | martyr | Rome | |
| 14 Sep | Cornelius and Cyprian | *c.* 258 | pope and martyr<br>martyr | Rome<br>Carthage | CT |
| 16 | Euphemia, Lucy, and Geminian | ? | martyrs | Chalcedon | |
| 29 | Michael | | archangel | | CT |
| 7 Oct | Mark | 336 | pope, not martyr | Rome | D |
| 14 | Callistus | *c.* 222 | pope and martyr | Rome | T |
| 1 Nov | Caesarius | ? | martyr | Terracina | |
| 8 | The Four Crowned Ones | 306? | martyrs | Rome | D |
| 21 | Cecilia | ? | martyr | Rome | CDT |
| 23 | Clement | 1st cent. | pope and martyr | Rome | CT |
| | Felicitas | ? | martyr | Rome | |
| 24 | Chrysogonus | 304? | martyr | Aquileia | CD |
| 29 | Saturninus | ? | martyr | Rome | |
| 29, 30 | Andrew | 1st cent. | apostle and martyr | (biblical) | CT |
| 13 Dec | Lucy | 304? | martyr | Syracuse | CT |
| 27 | John | 1st cent. | apostle | (biblical) | CDT |
| 28 | The Holy Innocents | 1st cent. | martyrs | (biblical) | T |

C: Named in the Roman canon
D: Patron saint of one of the earliest Roman churches
T: Still named in the roman calendar today, though not necessarily on the same date

Very few of these entries cause any problems. The majority of saints named are martyrs of Rome before the year 310. Even those who do not have a church dedicated in their honour probably first appeared in the calendar at the time of the anniversary Eucharists in the cemeteries. Of the nine days on which saints definitely associated with cities other than Rome are commemorated, a simple explanation is forthcoming for most. Agatha of Sicily and Gervasius and Protasius of Milan were sufficiently local for a cult to develop naturally. Chrysogonus of Aquileia has already been explained.[45] Agapitus of Palestrina possibly came into prominence if his name was associated with Pope Agapitus who died in 536. An oratory in Rome was built in honour of the saint by Felix III. Euphemia of Chalcedon became important when the church dedicated in her honour in the city of her martyrdom was used for the meetings of the Council of Chalcedon in 451. Some 160 years later the relics of Euphemia were transferred to a new church built in her honour in Rome. Caesarius of Terracina also achieved prominence because a church, the imperial chapel, was named after him by Valentinian III, an example of a saint with a suitable name being chosen as a patron. Caesarius was the obvious patron for the chapel of the Caesars. Felix of Nola, who is mentioned in the sixth-century Carthaginian martyrology, is one of the few saints in the calendar who were never said to have been martyred. But Paulinus of Nola had written of his sanctity and a cult had developed. A church was named in his honour in Rome sometime before the eighth century, and probably considerably earlier. Only two of the nine non-Roman saints provide problems. Of Lucy of Syracuse it is known that a church was named in her honour in the eighth century, yet because she is named in the Roman canon, she must have been venerated in Rome from an early date. We do not know why. Cyprian, a Carthaginian martyr, was commemorated with his great rival, Pope Cornelius. Cornelius provided the site for the celebration (at his tomb) while Cyprian provided the date (that of his martyrdom), a rather strange development.

The choice of biblical saints is interesting. The maryrdom of John the Baptist, Stephen, and the Holy Innocents is recorded in the New Testament. Peter and Paul were both associated with Rome and their martyrdom there was never in dispute. Michael the archangel is of course rather a special figure, attached to no particular community, but venerated in Rome apparently even before the dedication in his honour of a basilica on the *Via Solaris*. The other four, John, Andrew, James the Less, and Philip, are among the more prominent apostles, ones about whom there were ample gospel passages for liturgical reading.

The early Roman calendar gives us a picture of the earliest criteria for inclusion in the calendar. Sanctity in any vague sense is not one of them, but martyrdom is. The chief reasons are essentially local and practical—tombs at which to celebrate the Eucharist, relics to venerate, church dedications to observe. To say that inclusion in the calendar was a matter of luck would only be a small exaggeration, particularly as it was the Roman calendar that gradually gained universal acceptance in the churches of the west, so that Saint Praxedis, about whom nothing is known, was still being commemorated liturgically and all but universally into the second half of the twentieth century.

## vi

Felix, Marcellus, and Mark are the only non-biblical saints in the earliest Roman calendar who were not martyrs. Felix certainly suffered for the faith. During the persecution initiated in 250 by the emperor Decius he was arrested and treated with much brutality. But his fame grew because Paulinus of Nola, two hundred years later, built a church in his honour and wrote about him as a man who refused the office of a bishop and lived out his life as a simple priest, revered for his goodness and his sufferings under persecution. Marcellus and Mark were both popes and lived a little later than the other saints in the Roman calendar. Marcellus died in 309 and gave his name to the *titulus Marcelli.* Mark, who died in 336, built two churches, both called after his name, in one of which he was buried. The other was the *titulus Marci.* In an age that set such store upon martyrdom, it is strange that these three men should find a place in the calendar. It would be possible to argue that Marcellus and Mark found a place because of the sanctity of their lives, for once the persecutions were over, sanctity of life began to qualify a man or woman for commemoration in the calendar as much as martyrdom. But the more likely explanation is that they were commemorated simply because they had given their names to two of the *tituli.* Nevertheless, bishops, who were not martyrs, especially those who had been banished on account of their fidelity to the faith and had died in banishment, began to be regarded as saints worthy of commemoration. John Chrysostom represents the soul of Melitius, Bishop of Antioch, as 'dwelling in the celestial tabernacles' and aiding the prayers of the faithful members of his flock with God.[46] Felix, no doubt, was considered worthy of commemoration because his sufferings made him all but a martyr. He had suffered with his Lord and that could not go unrewarded. One of the most famous of the very early bishops to be venerated as a saint was Martin of Tours, who died in 397. Sulpitius Severus writes of him:

> Although the character of our times could not ensure him the honour of martyrdom, yet he will not remain destitute of the glory of a martyr, because by both vow and virtues he was alike able and willing to be a martyr.[47]

There was another category of saints who, as heroic death gave way to holy living in an age without persecution, came to be represented in the calendar. These were the ascetics and the religious. It was the remarkable growth of monasticism that drew attention to the fathers of the desert. Their carefully documented lives described miracles and acts of enduranсc, all consecrated by a life of virginity, which from the beginning the church had held to be particularly virtuous. Their relics and tombs came to be honoured in much the same way as those of the martyrs. Saint Gregory of Nyssa recounts a story of a man called Ephraem who invoked his patron saint, Saint Ephraem of Syria. The man was in great danger, asked the saint to come to his aid, and was saved on the spot.[48] Ephraem had been a theologian and a poet, but had not been martyred. Indeed he suffered little persecution. His vocation was to the ascetic life and, like his famous contemporary, Antony of Egypt, was accorded the honour previously given only to the martyrs. For, as the *Life of Antony,* a mid-fourth-century document, asserts:

> even if they work secretly, even if they wish to remain in obscurity, yet the Lord shows them as lamps to lighten all, that those who hear may thus know that the precepts of God are able to make men prosper and thus be zealous in the paths of virtue.[49]

This extension, whereby apostles, prophets, bishops, and ascetics were brought into the company of the martyrs as the exceptions to the rule that consigned the departed to Hades to await the judgement, was nevertheless illogical. The theological explanation that had seen martyrdom as the equivalent of baptism had allowed that one exception to exist alongside the general rule without contradiction. But the extension to categories who had not been 'baptized' with blood or fire introduced an inconsistency that inevitably speeded up the process that separated the saint from the rest of the departed and led to the formulation of very precise but quite unjustified doctrines about the status of the various categories of dead.

One further exception remains. Devotion to Mary, the mother of Jesus, developed quite early, but it seems to have taken a longer time to find liturgical expression in Rome. Gregory of Nazianzus tells of a virgin, Justina, who, 'beseeching the virgin Mary to help a virgin in danger', was delivered from peril.[50] Gregory saw nothing improbable about a story of a Christian in the first half of the third century seeking the aid of the mother of Jesus. The title *theotokos* was in use by the fourth century and the theologians of the time were not hesitant to speak of Mary as 'the new Eve' and 'the mother of God'. Pictures in the catacombs show an early devotion. But the doctrine of the bodily assumption is comparatively late. No scholars would date it before the fourth century in the west. This is surprising, for a doctrine of the assumption would have provided an explanation of how Mary, who was not a martyr, came to be in heaven. But, by the time the doctrine of the assumption was emerging, Christian theologians had ceased to believe that martyrdom was a precondition of entry into heaven in advance of the general judgement. No feasts of Mary are found in the earliest Roman calendar, except the Presentation, which is principally a feast of the Lord. The Assumption, the Nativity, and the Annunciation, coming from the Greek or Byzantine churches, did not establish themselves until the seventh century. But, before that time, 1 January, was kept in honour of Mary. There seems to be little doubt that both popular devotion and theological reflection about her placed her in heaven with her son, even if this meant an inconsistency in Christian eschatology. It was inconceivable that the *theotokos* should be denied the privileges of the martyrs.

## vii

There was only one voice of dissent as the doctrine of the saints developed. Vigilantius of Calagurris in Aquitaine attacked the veneration of martyrs. We have no record of what Vigilantius said, and have to rely on Jerome's reply to draw up a picture of his objections. He attacked the veneration paid to relics and to tombs. He objected to vigils and liturgical celebrations in the churches erected over the graves. He denied the power of the prayers of the saints, refusing to believe that the departed could have any interest at all in earthly affairs because they were all, saints or otherwise, in the underworld. Jerome, by way of reply, ascribed to the souls of the saints a kind of omnipresence or, at the very least, a capacity to transport themselves with incredible speed to various places.[51]

Vigilantius stood alone. Ranged on the side of Jerome were the great teachers of east and west—Basil, Gregory of Nazianzus, John Chrysostom, Ambrose, Augustine—all of whom agreed with Hilary[52] that the faithful were right to pray at the tombs of the saints and to venerate their relics and that such devotion would lead and did lead to miracles, such as the casting out of devils, recovery from sickness, escape from great dangers, and even raising of the dead.

# 2 *Centuries of Consolidation*

## i

The five centuries that intervene between the first creative period, that of the early Church, and the second recognised creative period, that of the medieval Church, were not stagnant years. Despite talk of 'dark ages', the Church of the year 1100 was by no means identical to that of the year 500. There was both theological and liturgical development. Nevertheless these were chiefly centuries of consolidation.

By the fourth century a theological view of the role of the saints had been developed that would need no further modification until such time as men's views of heaven, hell, and judgement were changed significantly. The fourth century knew no precisely defined doctrine of purgatory. Such a doctrine was of course already developing. The prayer of the imprisoned Perpetua for her dead brother, Dinocrates,[1] shows a trace of such a belief. Augustine held that the fate of the individual soul is decided immediately after death and taught the absolute certainty of purifying pains in the next life.[2] In the sixth century Christian thinkers, such as Caesarius of Arles, were beginning to make a distinction between capital sins, which led inevitably to hell, and minor ones, which could be expurgated either by good works on earth or in purgatory. This however was not sufficiently precise a doctrine to dismiss the majority of the departed as beyond the pale, outside the hearing of our prayers and unable to pray for us. The 'communion of saints' could continue to imply a mutuality of love and prayer across the barriers of death without too much need to define any more precisely the difference in status between the 'saints' and the remainder of the departed. The liturgical practice of the Church through the latter centuries of the first millenium reflected this sort of fluidity of belief within certain prescribed limits.

But even in an allegedly uncreative period, theology did not stand still. Gradually purgatory became more and more carefully defined. Augustine's work was to become the foundation of the medieval doctrine. Increasingly a need was felt to evolve the doctrine in such a way as to avoid a confusion of thought about the state of the souls between death and the last judgement. Evidence of this is to be found in the form of commemoration of the departed that came to be included during these centuries in the Roman canon of the Mass. Its existence, in very much the form that gained universal recognition, in the *Bobbio Missal*, which comprises eighth-century liturgical texts, points to the fact that by then, if not before, prayer for the departed and commemoration of the saints had become quite distinct. The prayer for the departed in the Roman canon is this:

> Remember also, Lord, the names of those who have gone before us with the sign of faith, and sleep in the sleep of peace. We beseech you to grant them and to all who rest in Christ a place of restoration, light, and peace.

But in commemoration of the saints it prays:

> To us sinners, your servants also, who trust in the multitude of your mercies, vouchsafe to grant some part and fellowship with your holy apostles and martyrs: with John, Stephen, Matthias, Barnabas, Ignatius, Alexander, Marcellinus, Peter, Felicity, Perpetua, Agatha, Lucy, Agnes, Cecilia, Anastasia, and with all your saints: into whose company, we ask that you will admit us, not weighing our merit, but bounteously forgiving through Christ our Lord.

Liturgy was expressing the Christian belief in this way by the eighth century, but it was not until the thirteenth century that the doctrine was fully amplified by Thomas Aquinas[3] and defined by the Church at the Council of Lyons in 1274. Until that time, and therefore throughout the period now under examination, a variety of attitudes were possible, though an increasingly formalised method of canonisation hastened the end of any such variety.

## ii

The making of a saint was at first a spontaneous act of a local community. But it was not long before such canonisation by acclamation had to be brought under control. The latter half of the first millenium marks a period of increasing control by authorities—episcopal, synodical, and papal—over the process until in the twelfth century nothing less than papal approval, given after much evidence and then only if political circumstances were right, would suffice.

The first move towards episcopal control belongs to the fourth century when Augustine complained about his Donatist opponents who actually sought martyrdom:

> Some went so far as to offer themselves for slaughter to any travellers whom they met with arms, using violent threats that they would murder them if they failed to meet death at their hands. Sometimes, too, they extorted with violence from any passing judge that they should be put to death by the executioners, or by the officer of his court ... Again it was their daily sport to kill themselves, by throwing themselves over precipices, or into the water, or into the fire.[4]

The first Council of Carthage in 348 tried to put a stop to such behaviour and Bishop Optatus, about twenty years later, argued that a true martyrdom must be preceded by the confession of the name of Christ and must be built on the foundation of the love of peace.[5] The problem continued for a century and bishops were empowered to destroy any shrine where they were convinced that no true saint was venerated. But after the end of the fourth century, matters were made more complicated by invasion. Tombs and relics were destroyed and, when not actually destroyed, translated. The arrival of a relic of some Christian hero of another city or country provided a local bishop with a problem in an age when local commemoration was the norm. This translation process, which grew from the sixth century, had the effect of giving to the commemoration of some of the saints a universal observance. The same period saw the spread of calendars from one city or country to another and particularly the ascendancy of the Roman calendar and the Roman saints, though the influence of Gaul on liturgical practices (even in Rome) was almost as great. By the eighth century, the translation of a saint was regarded as an act of canonisation. This normally involved reburying the saint above ground. It came to be considered improper for a saint to be buried underground. But this was not a spontaneous reburial by the community, but a solemn liturgical act presided over by the bishop, who sometimes would refuse to take part in such a ceremony, if he doubted the sanctity of the hero concerned.

Sometimes a bishop made a decision alone, but it seems to have been customary for such solemn decisions to be made in synod.

One such synod was that which met at Clovesho (probably near Rochester) in 747. This was a synod of the church in southern England. It promulged a canon which ordered the observance in England of a feast to commemorate Archbishop Augustine of Canterbury. Until that date Augustine does not seem to have been regarded as a saint. Bede in 734 refers to him as 'the blessed archbishop Augustine' and Boniface calls him 'the first preacher of the English' in a letter in which he frequently calls Pope Gregory a 'saint'.[6] And yet alongside this picture of formal canonisation by decree, there still seems to have been canonisation by the spontaneous act of the local community where no controversy was involved. Despite the Council of Clovesho, many British saints would seem to have been venerated simply because of local enthusiasm. Usually their commemoration became national or even universal in time. Saint Wilfrid of Ripon, for instance, was venerated in the north of England, where he had been bishop, very soon after his death. An annual commemoration was held at Ripon where he was buried. It seems to have been observed, not because of any synodical or episcopal decision, but because one of his disciples, an abbot, resolved to celebrate each week the day on which he died as a feast as though it were a Sunday.[7] Out of that weekly celebration grew the annual observance that within a century had spread throughout the land. Other local commemorations however never won national observance and the local hero was not recognised as a saint. A fascinating entry in an eleventh-century calendar, obviously of Wessex origin, records for 26 October the observance of '*Sancti Eadfridi confessoris*'.[8] This is the traditional date of the death in 889 of King Alfred. It would therefore appear that at least one community happily commemorated this Christian king as 'Saint Alfred', even though there had been no official canonisation and though the cult of Alfred did not spread.

Interference by the bishop seems to have been restricted as a general rule to occasions when it was necessary to stamp out an undesirable cult or when the bishop desired to give greater status to a local cult hero by adding his episcopal approval to the community's acclamation. There is evidence from the tenth century of bishops acting together to canonise. There is evidence too from the time of Charlemagne of a part played in the process of canonisation by secular authority. It was not often a very significant role, although in England in 980 the body of the murdered King Edward was translated to Shaftesbury, where the tomb became a scene of pilgrimage, and the observance of the day of Edward's 'martyrdom' was ordered in 1008 by King Ethelred and his council, the Witan.[9] After the tenth century, episcopal canonisation gives way, as a general rule, to papal canonisation. At the very end of the period under discussion, the body of King Edward the Confessor was translated in a ceremony over which Gundulf, Bishop of Rochester, presided. Episcopal presidency at a translation, which a century or so before would have constituted canonisation, clearly no longer did so. For in 1138 Pope Innocent III was asked to canonise Edward. That he would have assented were it not for civil war in England between Stephen and Matilda, in which he did not want to become involved, is fairly certain. But he refused to act, asking the abbot and monks of Westminster to produce more evidence that there was widespread demand in England for the canonisation. Fifty years later, apparently without any such assurance, Pope Alexander III canonised Edward. The development of the idea of papal canonisation was a natural offshoot of the growth of the power and prestige of the Roman Church from the eleventh century onwards. For a time papal canonisation was but one of several methods and the pope, as much as any other bishop, consulted fellow bishops and synods. But increasingly the stage was being set for canonisation, on the evidence of miracles as well as biographies and popular acclaim, by the decision of one man, acting alone, the role of the community or the bishop being reduced to that of presenting a case. But the story of papal control belongs to the Middle Ages, rather than to the dark centuries of consolidation, when not only canonisation but the eschatological view from which it had to emerge would be given an exactness and an inflexibility that the first thousand years of Christianity had not known.

## iii

In the English church of this time were observed saints from many nations. The liturgical influences in England seem to have come from many different areas. There was of course in the north a Christian tradition that had been isolated from Roman influence. But Roman practices spread fast not only in the south, where Augustine and his fellow missionaries under the Roman obedience preached, but also in the north, where Wilfrid and

Benedict Biscop embraced the Roman way enthusiastically. But pre-conquest calendars in England contain many foreign names other than those of Rome. Italian influence was not restricted to Rome. The old *English Martyrology*,[10] which has survived in a ninth century Mercian form, includes a host of Italian saints mainly associated with Naples. The influence of Gaul was also clearly and understandably strong. The martyrology is an interesting document. There are very few southern English saints in it, but Alban, Ethelburga, and Augustine merit entries. There is of course no definitive calendar for the pre-conquest church. Each diocese or great church had its own, though most conformed to a pattern. The different ways in which Augustine, Wilfrid, and Alfred found their way into some of these calendars has already been described.[11] An examination of all the extant tenth and eleventh century English calendars reveals that apart from all the observances shared with churches of the continent, twelve British saints were commemorated throughout the land or over a very wide part of it.

| | | |
|---|---|---|
| 29 Jan | Gildas the Wise, monk and writer (*c.* 570) | |
| 20 Mar | Cuthbert, Bishop of Lindisfarne, missionary (687) | A |
| 11 Apr | Guthlac of Crowland, hermit (714) | |
| 26 May | Augustine, first Archbishop of Canterbury, missionary (605) | A R |
| 5 Jun | Boniface of Crediton, Bishop of Mainz, missionary and martyr (755) | A R |
| 22 | Alban, first martyr of Britain (*c.* 304) | A R |
| 23 | Etheldreda, queen, abbess of Ely (679) | A |
| 17 Jul | Kenelm of Winchcombe, prince, martyr (*c.* 811) | |
| 5 Aug | Oswald, King of Northumbria, martyr (642) | A |
| 10 Oct | Paulinus, Bishop of York and of Rochester (644) | |
| 12 | Wilfrid of Ripon, Bishop of York and of Hexham (709) | |
| 3 Dec | Birinus, Bishop of Dorchester, missionary (650) | |

A Commemorated today in the Church of England (1662 *Book of Common Prayer* or 1928 proposed *Book of Common Prayer*)

R Commemorated today in the Roman Catholic Church in England (National Calendar for England)

Boniface was canonised in the same way as Augustine, by action of a synod in 755 almost straight after his martyrdom. Alban, like Augustine, is mentioned in the old English Martyrology. Cuthbert's body was removed from its grave in 698, only eleven years after his death, and placed in a chest above the floor. This was done by decision of the monks of Durham and after the approval of their bishop, Eadberct.[12] This was another case of local community veneration. Cuthbert is mentioned in the eighth-century calendar and martyrology of Saint Willibrord, a specially interesting document in that it includes saintly figures whom Willibrord himself had known, his own father among them. King Oswald receives a mention in it. His presence in the calendars of the time is not surprising. He was a martyr and English martyrs were rare. Bede bore witness to the sanctity of his life.[13] The presence of Paulinus and Birinus is also no surprise. Figures rather like Augustine and Wilfrid, they had had great influence over the church in the area in which they had presided and, as missionary bishops, were looked back to very much as founders of the faith in particular places. Gildas, called 'The Wise' as Bede was called 'The Venerable', was, like Bede, a historical writer of a rather moralising kind. But the popularity throughout the land of Etheldreda, the virgin queen twice married, Kenelm, the young Mercian prince done to death, and Guthlac, the hermit around whose tomb Crowland Abbey was built, is less easy to understand. Most of these commemorations no doubt began as local ones, of which that of Wilfrid is an example. Probably Augustine and Boniface were the only two to receive synodical canonisation. But by the end of the tenth century they were all well established throughout the land, though our evidence for the north of England is sufficiently limited that these conclusions can be advanced only very tentatively with regard to practice north of the Humber.

A rather larger group of British saints achieved a fair degree of recognition. They were honoured in several communities and not just in one rather restricted geographical area. Such was English religious history that there was hardly a martyr among them, but monks and nuns feature prominently in the list.

| | | | |
|---|---|---|---|
| 13 Feb | Ermenilda, queen, abbess of Ely (*c.* 700) | | |
| 2 Mar | Chad, Bishop of Lichfield, missionary (672) | A | |
| 17 | Patrick, missionary bishop among the Irish (*c.* 461) | A | R |
| 18 | Edward, King of the West Saxons, martyr (978)[14] | A | |
| 24 Apr | Mellitus, Bishop of London and Archbishop of Canterbury (624) | | |
| 30 | Erconwald, Bishop of London (*c.* 693) | | |
| 19 May | Dunstan, Archbishop of Canterbury (988) | A | |
| 25 | Aldhelm, Bishop of Sherborne, missionary (709) | A | |
| 15 Jun | Edburga, abbess of Winchester (960) | | |

| | | |
|---|---|---|
| 2 Jul | Swithun, Bishop of Winchester (862) | A |
| 6 | Sexburga, queen, abbess of Minster-in-Sheppey and of Ely (*c.* 699) | |
| 8 | Grimbald, abbot of Winchester (903) | |
| 13 | Mildred, abbess of Minster-in-Thanet (*c.* 700) | |
| 28 | Samson, Welsh abbot and missionary (*c.* 656) | |
| 31 | German, Bishop of Auxerre, missionary (488) | |
| 31 Aug | Aidan, Bishop of Lindisfarne, missionary (651) | A |
| 19 Sep | Theodore of Tarsus, Archbishop of Canterbury (690) | A |
| 25 | Ceolfrid, abbot of Jarrow (716) | |
| 11 Oct | Ethelburga, abbess of Barking (*c.* 676) | |
| 3 Nov | Rumwald of Brackley, priest (date unknown) | |
| 10 | Justus, Bishop of Rochester and Archbishop of Canterbury (627) | |

Perhaps the most striking fact about these commemorations is how few of them are observed today. Heroic figures like Grimbald and Edburga of Winchester so impressed their contemporaries that, within a few years of their death, they were incorporated into the calendar. Their contemporaries found in them something that marked them out, whether their holiness or their courage or whatever. But their attraction for the Christians of their own century did not guarantee them a permanent place in the devotion of English Christians. The England of the Dark Ages was soon left behind by the strange new world of the Middle Ages where saints of a very different kind, not the monks and missionaries of those earlier times, but bishops and statesmen, like Hugh of Lincoln, Richard of Chichester, and Edmund of Canterbury, aroused feelings of admiration and devotion. But this same world of the Middle Ages brought the first protests against the doctrines on which the commemoration of saints was based.

# 3 *Medieval Certainty*

i

The Middle Ages brought with them not so much a new doctrine or even an old doctrine further developed, but a clarification, a richer presentation, and a uniformity of the doctrine that had developed through the years from the patristic age to the age of Aquinas. There was a clarification because no theologian, not even Augustine, had set out a Christian view of heaven, hell, and purgatory, and a view of saints that accorded with it, in such a systematic, precise, and defined way as Thomas Aquinas was to do in the thirteenth century. There was a richness of presentation in that the doctrine defined by Aquinas became the subject of literature of at least two types. There were the devotional writings of such people as (in England) Anselm of Canterbury[1] and Julian of Norwich,[2] but, on a far higher literary plane, there was Dante's *Divina Commedia.*[3] Doctrinally, this fourteenth-century poet is at one with Aquinas, but the language that he employs lifts the medieval view of heaven, hell, and purgatory from the prosaic language of doctrinal definition to the language of art and literature. There was a uniformity to the doctrine as now presented in that the illogicalities and differences of interpretation already noted were ironed out or swept away.

Thomas Aquinas believed that a man lives on after his death in a variety of different ways. He wrote:

> Although a man's personal career ends with death, his life goes on in a sense, and is affected by what happens afterwards. He lives on in men's memories . . . He lives on also in his children, who, so to speak, are part of their parents . . . He survives in the results of his actions . . . He continues in his body, sometimes given honourable burial, sometimes left unburied, but always eventually crumbling into dust. Finally, he lasts in the projects upon which he had set his heart, which sometimes come to quick failure and sometimes endure longer. All these affairs are submitted to Divine Judgement, but a full and perfect verdict cannot be pronounced and sentence passed

while time rolls on its course. How right and proper, then, a final judgement on the last day, when everything whatsoever about a man will be manifestly displayed.[4]

A final judgement at the end of time is therefore important. But the moment of death has now become an equally important moment for the soul's destiny. Thomas taught that the guilt (*culpa*) of venial sin is expiated immediately after death by an act of perfect charity and that only the pain remains to be borne. He asserted that Jesus Christ descended to the place of the damned after the crucifixion. This is how he interprets the words of the First Epistle of Peter:

> In the body he was put to death; in the spirit he was brought to life. And in the spirit he went and made his proclamation to the imprisoned spirits. They had refused obedience long ago . . . Why was the gospel preached to those who are dead? In order that, although in the body they received the sentence common to men, they might in the spirit be alive with the life of God.[5]

Aquinas believes that this passage indicates not merely a visit to Hades, the place of the dead, but to the place of the damned. And, arising from such a view, the 'harrowing of hell' came to occupy an important place in the medieval imagination. In art and in drama, it came to be conceived, despite the biblical emphasis, as a rescue operation, releasing from hell those who did not deserve to be there. These were chiefly the heroes of the Old Testament. But the real emphasis of the writer of the epistle is that the disobedient, not the patriarchs, are given a second chance. This emphasis was ignored or misunderstood by the medieval church, the principal interest of Thomas and the other scholastic theologians being not in any thought of a second chance for those in hell but in the final salvation of those in purgatory. They believed that the smallest pain in purgatory was greater than the greatest pain on earth. The pain was relieved, however, by the certainty of salvation which upheld the suffering souls and kept them faithful, and even in deep peace, despite their sufferings. Furthermore they could be aided and relieved by the prayers of the living on earth, particularly by the offering of the Eucharist on their behalf, a belief which Thomas bases on the doctrine of the communion of saints, a fellowship from which only the inhabitants of hell and of limbo are excluded. Thomas's view was in part a result of the great shift in pastoral practice in the sixth century which had replaced public confession and absolution after penance by private confession and absolution before penance, leading inevitably to the medieval idea of purgatory as the place where the tariff of temporal suffering imposed by God on the remitting of venial sins, as yet unpaid, would be worked off. It followed naturally from that view that the offering of prayers and of the Eucharist by the living on behalf of the dead in purgatory could shorten their stay there.

But, though Thomas saw this as a consequence of a belief in the communion of saints, it was a very lopsided view of that doctrine. Gone was the mutuality and reciprocity of the earlier patristic view in which living prayed for dead and dead for living. The Middle Ages followed the very late patristic outlook in restricting invocation to the canonised saints. Thomas repudiated the idea that the souls in purgatory could offer prayers on the grounds that 'they do not yet enjoy the vision of the Word'[6] and believed that 'they are not in a condition of offering prayer'.[7] He is however quite confident of the prayers, not only of the living, but also of the canonised saints, for the souls in purgatory:

> It is manifest that they know in the Word the vows and devotions and prayers of men who seek their aid . . . God alone knows of himself the thoughts of the hearts, but nonetheless others know them in so far as revelation is made to them either by the vision of the Word or in some other way.[8]

He clearly makes a distinction between prayers to God and prayers to the saints, although this distinction is not always apparent in the medieval prayers even of orthodox and educated Christians. The distinction cannot be made much more explicit however than when he asserts that

> we seek from the Holy Trinity that God may have mercy upon us; we seek from whatever saints we address that they pray for us . . . The petitions that we direct to them they know by the manifestation of God.[9]

The views that Thomas held were those of the medieval church as a whole and were confirmed at both the Second Council of Lyons in 1274 and also at the Council of Florence in 1439. Controversy had arisen between the Greek and Latin churches on the doctrine of purgatory and the consequences of it. Though both sides believed in prayers for the dead, the Greeks regarded the universal last judgement as of supreme importance and therefore tended to attach far less weight than theologians like Thomas did to the moment of death. They believed that the good and the evil were still essentially in the same place. For the only fire was to be that of the last judgement. The saints had already been purified (but not of course by fire). Nevertheless even they, including Mary and the apostles, had to undergo the final judgement. The compromise that was reached at the councils (though it appears to be all but an outright victory for the Latin view, for the Greeks accepted with reservation the dogma of the particular judgement after death) preserved a tension that outlived the medieval period between the competing claimants for the title of 'moment of judgement'—the death of the Christian and the end of the world.

## ii

Devotion to the saints arising out of this medieval view of eschatology varied considerably. Some of it was ill-informed and was quite unjustifiable. It was bad theology. But even the prayers of informed Christians showed a lack of consistency and a failure to follow entirely the view that the Church was in the process of endorsing. A particular problem was the question of the sort of prayer that it was appropriate to offer to the saints. In a prayer to Mary, the mother of Jesus, Anselm, the eleventh-century Archbishop of Canterbury and theologian, writing of course before Thomas Aquinas, prays:

> God, who was made the son of a woman out of mercy;
> woman, who was made mother of God out of mercy;
> have mercy upon this wretch,
> you forgiving, you interceding.[10]

Though God and Mary are linked together and the mercy of both is sought, the distinction is clear. God's mercy will be revealed in forgiving Anselm, Mary's simply in praying for Anselm to God. It is the same distinction that Thomas Aquinas makes when he says that from God we seek mercy but from the saints that they pray for us.[11] Anselm shows the same grasp of the different sorts of prayer appropriate when he prays to God and to John the Baptist:

> Behold, healer, and the healer's witness, here am I—
> behold, the sick servant of the healer and his work

> petitions here the healer and his witness.
> True healer, I pray you heal me;
> true witness, I beg you to pray for me.
> Reconcile me to myself,
> you by your actions, you by your words.[12]

This is, by the standards set by Thomas Aquinas, a model prayer. The distinction is finely but clearly drawn—precisely what one would expect of a theologian of Anselm's ability and precision. All the more surprising is it, therefore, to find him praying in quite a different way to Mary:

> Most gentle Lady, heal my weakness,
> and you will be taking away the filth that offends you.
> Most kind Lady, take away my sickness,
> and you will not experience the dirt you shudder at.
> Most dear Lady, do not let what grieves you be,
> and there will be nothing to defile your holiness.
> Hear me, Lady,
> and make whole the soul of a sinner who is your servant.[13]

Though some of this is ambiguous, it seems to stray beyond the point where only the intercession of the saint is sought. There is at least a hint of the ability of the saint to grant requests beyond the mere promise of prayer. This is probably to be seen not so much as the outcome of a different theological view point, for we are dealing with the same theologian who in other places is so careful to make the very distinction that he fails to make here, but as another example of the devotion of the soul, carried along by love and yearning, failing to take account of theological orthodoxy as the emotional takes over from the intellectual. If we find that in Anselm the great theologian, how much more we shall expect to find it in the devotional practices of the less sophisticated. And so it was that, as far as the ordinary medieval Christian was concerned, the importance of the saints lay not in the belief that the holy men and women of the past had exemplified an ideal code of moral conduct, nor yet that their prayers to God were received with particular favour, but that they could themselves employ supernatural powers to relieve the sins and sufferings of the living, or at least of so many of the living as prayed to them.

The ordinary Christian prayed to the saints because he expected to see a result—nothing less than a miracle, stories of which abounded. Such miracles did not belong only to the distant past. It was a faith not in miracles that had once happened but in miracles that might happen at any moment. The 'lives' of the saints concentrated far more on the power of their heroes to perform miracles than on qualities of heroism or sanctity. The saints were also said to prophesy the future, to control the weather, to give protection against fire and flood, to transport magically heavy objects and, of course, to heal the sick. Most popular of these 'lives' were those recounted in *The Golden Legend*, a thirteenth-century Italian document, translated by Caxton in 1483 and popular in England in the last decades before the Reformation.[14]

However much theologians might assert that the saints were only intercessors, whose prayers need not necessarily be heeded, Christian people offered prayers expecting much more, and the Church did very little to check this. Indeed in places it encouraged such practices, for there were vested interests that could benefit from the foolishness of the unsophisticated. The great shrine of Mary at Walsingham, of Thomas Becket at Canterbury, of Edward the Confessor at Westminster, and of Alban, the first British martyr, at St. Albans, drew pilgrims in their thousands and the business fortunes of many depended on the continuation of such practices. Chaucer's portrayal of the journey to Canterbury of a group of pilgrims to the shrine of Saint Thomas amply shows both the mixed motives of the participants and the number of those whose life and livelihood was bound up with such things.[15] Associated with shrines were the relics of the saints, very often not authentic, in which there was a busy trade because they were believed to have the power to cure illness and to protect against danger. Images served the same purpose. What a long way from Thomas Aquinas's view of the saints in heaven as intercessors is this picture of statues on earth magically granting favours, such as the statue in St Paul's Cathedral of Saint Wilgerfort which would eliminate the husbands of those discontented wives who chose to offer a peck of oats.[16] For, whether saints or only their statues, the holy dead were believed to be able not only to send healing and to do good, but to cause great trouble for those who did not treat them with the respect they deserved. No wonder that William Tyndale, that early Protestant martyr, could complain on the eve of the Reformation, that

> we worship saints for fear, lest they should be displeased and angry with us, and plague us or hurt us; as who is not afraid of Saint

> Laurence? Who dare deny Saint Antony a fleece of wool for fear of his terrible fire, or lest he send the pox among our sheep?[17]

Protest was inevitable. But the scene was not uniformly black. There survived, at least among some, a more acceptable view of saints that saw them for what they had been on earth and for what, entirely by the grace of God, they now were in heaven. Julian of Norwich, the fourteenth-century mystic, saw in one of her visions Saint John of Beverley, a seventh-century saint who was very popular in medieval England and to whom were attributed a great many miracles. Julian, in recording her vision, however, does not dwell long on the miraculous, but speaks chiefly of his sanctification which, among all the abuse of the veneration of saints that surrounded her, quite understandably makes her 'glad and cheerful and loving':

> Saint John of Beverley our Lord showed vividly, a comfort to us because he was so homely and unaffected, which brought to mind the fact that he was a neighbour and acquaintance. God called him, most happily, 'Saint John of Beverley' just as we do, showing that he sees him as an exalted saint in heaven, and blessed. At the same time he mentioned that in his young and tender years he was a very dear servant of God, loving and fearing God very greatly. Yet God allowed him to fall, though in his mercy he kept him from perishing, and from losing ground. Afterwards God raised him to much greater grace, and because of the humility and contrition of his life, in heaven God has given him many joys, greater even than those he would have had had he never fallen. And God shows this to be true by the many and continuing miracles that are wrought by his body today.[18]

## iii

The protest that William Tyndale made belongs to the story of the Reformation. But, almost two centuries before, the voice of a near contemporary of Julian of Norwich launched an attack on the medieval Church. The voice of protest was that of John Wyclif. Writing in the middle of the fourteenth century, he attacked with vigour aspects of popular devotion to the saints, though he did not dispute the eschatological view of the medieval Church and defended the concept of purgatory. 'The Church,' he wrote, 'is threefold, of the triumphant in heaven; of the militant on earth; and of the sleepers in purgatory.'[19] He was simply following the orthodox catholic teaching of his time and, though his views on some matters changed and developed a good deal late in his life, on this point he seems to have remained consistent. In his early writings he also accepted a good deal of the medieval view of saints. Thus, in a sermon preached on the feast of the Assumption of Mary, he could write that

> Even fellow pilgrims upon earth, moved by brotherly love, help one another in the time of need, but the blessed virgin in heaven beholds our necessities, and is still more full of love, still richer in compassion; and all the more carefully does she care for our needs, as she knows that she has attained to so high honour in order that she might become the refuge of sinners.

This could as well have been written by Julian or Anselm. But, later in his life, Wyclif was to become increasingly doubtful about both the Church's right to canonise certain Christians and also the moral value of the devotions offered to saints. Expressing himself cautiously at first, in *De Civili Dominio*, he suggests the possibility (and no more than that) that the Church in its canonisations may deceive itself, whether through the love of money, or through love for the departed person, or through the mischief of the devil. He wonders whether there are not a good many holy monks who merit canonisation more than some of the saints. But that the Church would not have disputed. Nobody had ever claimed that the Church had identified every saint. But Wyclif concedes that somebody has to make the decision (and therefore that saints ought to be commemorated) and nobody but the Church can assume the role. In *De Ecclesia* he goes a little further and declares that

> certainly no Christian can believe that it is necessary to salvation to believe of this or that person whom the Church canonises that he is in glory on that account, especially in respect to certain modern saints.

He goes further in the *Trialogus* when he asserts it to be a blasphemous pretension to pronounce persons to be saints, when the Church cannot know the quality of their sanctity.[20] Although Wyclif went no further than to suggest that it was impossible without a special revelation for the papal curia to know whether a man were a saint or not, some of his followers did so. William White, who was burnt as a heretic in Norwich in 1428, believed that a canonisation could only be made by a general council. This at least is what the provincial of the English Carmelites,

Thomas Netter, who tried him, thought he believed and it was Netter's understanding that Wyclif himself had believed this too.[21]

As for commemorating these saints, Wyclif came to a position where, without condemning the practice outright, he saw so many dangers that there was little left to commend it. Devotion to a saint was only of value in so far as it promoted devotion to the Lord. Certainly there were too many saints' days:

> As the apostles, without any such saints' days, loved Jesus Christ more than we do, it appears to many orthodox Christians a rash and dangerous thing to institute so many saints' festivals, and they deem that it would be better not to have so many celebrations burdening the Church.

All too often their celebration was hardly a religious occasion but was of a very worldly character. The veneration of relics and the practice of going on pilgrimage did not excite from him as much opposition as might have been expected. But, though he is unwilling to condemn such things completely, neither is he very enthusiastic about them. For

> those who go on pilgrimage, worship relics, and collect money, might at least occupy themselves more usefully, if they omitted these practices. From the Word of God it even appears to be the duty of all such persons to employ themselves better at the present time.

There is a social side to Wyclif's objection, for he claims that it would be to the benefit of the Church, and to the honour of the saints, if the riches so foolishly lavished on the shrines were divided among the poor. As for prayer within the communion of saints, it is clear that Wyclif believes in the intercession of the saints for us, even claiming at one point that

> it seems to me to be impossible that we should obtain the reward without the help of Mary. . . . There is no sex or age, no rank or position of any one in the whole human race, which has no need to call for the help of the holy virgin.

But he has no great enthusiasm for prayers for the dead, believing that the good which a man does in his life time, however small, will be of more use to him at the judgement than the spending of many thousands of pounds by his executors after his death for the repose of his soul. Masses for the dead were not however condemned. In this, as in other aspects of eschatology, Wyclif remained more loyal to medieval religion than might have been expected from his forthright attacks on some other aspects of its belief, such as transubstantiation in eucharistic doctrine. A more thorough going attack on the whole concept of clearly defined distinctions between the dead who were saved, some being in heaven and some in purgatory, had to wait until the Reformation, though the seed of such a radical view was sown as early as the twelfth century by the Waldenses, a small sect of disputed origin who exercised some influence on the continent in the centuries of medieval decline.

## iv

The challenge to the Church in this area of belief and practice was not a serious one. The confidence of the Church in what it was doing was underlined by the further formalising of the process of canonisation. The process placed the decision more and more in the hands of the pope, particularly from the time of Alexander III, who reigned for twenty-two years from 1159, and who imposed the authority of his office on the process in a way that his predecessors had not quite managed to do. Certain of his right to control the veneration of any new saints, he made decisions about canonisations without reference to any formal body, though previously even the pope had only acted synodically. The formality involved now lay, not in the making of the decision, but in the presentation of the case. Canonisation became a long and expensive business and certain proofs were required beyond evidence of a holy life. Only miracles could indicate adequately that what had appeared to be a saintly life really had been one. Those who advocated the canonisation of a particular holy man or woman spent much money in sending to Rome and maintaining in Rome proctors to present the case. Papal authorisation was by now the norm, but there was still a degree of variety in the way that authority was exercised. When Archbishop Becket of Canterbury sent to the pope evidence of the holy life and miracles of his predecessor, the theologian Anselm, Alexander replied (after a long time) that the archbishop should call together a synod of bishops, abbots, and other church leaders in his province to decide whether Anselm should be canonised and Alexander promised to accept their decision. So papal authority was required, but it could be delegated to the extent of becoming little more than a formality.[22]

But when Archbishop Becket himself was murdered, the role of the pope in the canonisation process was rather different. At first he appeared to regard the death of Becket as an ordinary piece of violence, despite the outburst of popular devotion to his memory and the stories that circulated so quickly of miracles at his tomb. Clearly he was concerned with relations with Henry II, the English king, and it may have been this that prevented him from referring Becket's cause to the new archbishop in synod in England. Instead, after a delay that infuriated the English who already regarded the dead archbishop as a martyr, he himself made the decision and in 1173 sent the bull *Gaudendum est* to the chapter of Canterbury telling them that Becket was canonised and ordering them to translate his body and observe his feast.[23] But, despite their irritation at the delay, the churchmen in England do seem to have accepted that, without the approval of the pope, Becket could not be venerated as a saint.[24]

Despite this there is evidence of a continued cult of certain holy men who had not received papal recognition. The most famous English example of this was Robert Grosseteste, Bishop of Lincoln, who, like his successor, Bishop Dalderley, was venerated locally as a saint for many years while papal permission for the cult, never incidentally given, was awaited. The pope does not seem to have refused canonisation, but simply to have vacillated. The annals of Burton speak of the tomb of Saint Robert at which miracles were performed.[25] But Grosseteste does not seem to have been assigned a feast day and thus some distinction from a canonised saint was made. The cult was also restricted to Lincoln and it may well have been regarded simply as a local anticipation of the universal recognition from the pope that would be required before a feast day could be observed and its observance made widespread. Certainly, since the pope had not categorically refused the canonisation, the commemoration could not be regarded as a challenge to the pope's role in this sort of case. On the continent however there were just such challenges. For instance, the pope refused to canonise Antony Manzonius of Padua on the strange grounds that one Saint Antony was quite enough for Padua. But the cult went on with a feast day that was a public holiday and all sorts of local celebrations.[26]

There were therefore still limits to papal control. Such control, difficult in the case of canonisation itself, was all but impossible in the case of relics. Innocent III was particularly concerned about the sale of relics and about the abuse of exposing relics for money, especially new relics the authenticity of which was in grave doubt. Under his influence therefore the Fourth Lateran Council in 1215 ordered that old relics were only to be exposed in a reliquary and were not to be sold, and that no new relics were to be venerated without papal permission. In this area too, bishops were no longer to be trusted to make sensible decisions. As with saints, so now with their relics, the final word must come from the pope himself. This papal control of the whole area of the veneration of saints meant a great deal of formality and delay, except where a local cult was so strong that the conventions were ignored, so much so that in the case of the canonisation of Osmund, the eleventh-century Bishop of Sarum, that it was not until 1457 that Calixtus III declared Osmund a saint—a wait of over three hundred and fifty years. By the time that Osmund had been canonised, though the certainty of the Middle Ages looked firm, in England at least saints and their shrines had less than a hundred years of peace to enjoy. And even before that peace was shattered well-established beliefs were to be challenged forcefully on the continent in a far more fundamental way than John Wyclif and his early followers had done.

# 4 *Destruction and Reform*

i

John Calvin, replying in 1589 to a letter by Cardinal Jacob Sadolet to the senate and people of Geneva, seeking to recall them to loyalty to the Roman Catholic Church, saw in the doctrine of purgatory one of the foundation stones of the whole construction of medieval superstition and error:

> You yourself know what a hydra of errors thence emerged; you know what tricks superstition has spontaneously devised with which to play; . . . you know how great detriment it has done to piety. For not to mention how greatly true worship has in consequence decayed, the worst result certainly was that, while without command from God everyone competed with each other in helping the dead, they utterly neglected the proper offices of charity which are so strictly enjoined.[1]

This criticism belongs of course to a later stage in the Reformation process. Purgatory and doctrines that arise from it had been attacked throughout the previous half century, not least by Calvin himself. His systematic approach is found in the *Institutes* of 1536 and is in the main an attempt to refute the doctrine by his own exposition of the biblical passages often used to support it. The strength of his feeling on the matter, so strong that he believes that 'we must cry out with the shouting not only of our voices but of our throats and lungs that purgatory is a deadly fiction of Satan, which nullifies the cross of Christ,'[2] is dictated by his conviction that the doctrine implies that the expiation of sins is sought somewhere other than in the death of Jesus Christ, that sin is in fact paid for by the dead themselves in purgatory. He examines in turn every passage used in defence of purgatory and attempts to overturn the traditional interpretation in each case. In the gospels, for instance, he considers the advice of Jesus to those who are taken to court to settle quickly lest they be committed to prison where they will not be let out until they have paid the last penny.[3] His own explanation is that Jesus,

> in order to urge his followers more cogently to equity and concord, meant to show the many dangers and evils to which men expose themselves who obstinately prefer to demand the letter of the law rather than to act out of equity and goodness.[4]

Such an explanation, he believes, does away with any need for a doctrine of purgatory. In similar fashion he dismisses all the other texts in the New Testament that seem to support the idea of purgatory.

Calvin then turns his attention to prayers for the dead. He emphasises that there is no warrant for this in the New Testament and that even the early theologians who did justify such prayer recognised that they had no biblical authority for doing so. He explained their prayer in terms of emotion. It was not excusable, for they could not have had a clear conscience about it, but it was understandable, for

> they were seeking comfort to relieve their sorrow, and it seemed inhuman to them not to show before God some evidence of their love toward the dead. All men know by experience how man's nature is inclined to this feeling.[5]

Calvin was right in seeing a good deal of prayer for the dead in terms of this instinctive emotional need to express concern for the departed, but he does less than justice to early Christian theologians in imagining that their emotions were entirely out of step with their intellect. The historical development of the doctrine has been one of intellectual justification of this instinctive belief.

Because Calvin rejected the medieval view of purgatory, not surprisingly he was equally unsympathetic to the veneration of saints. His dislike reached its high point in describing the attitude of the clergy who, far from leading their people away from superstitious practices, encouraged them for reasons of financial gain, even when the people prayed to the saints 'not as helpers, but as determiners of their salvation'. Unenthusiastic about the prayers of the saints under any circumstances, Calvin was nevertheless willing to admit that in a certain sense the saints may pray for the living, and he was even able to say that a request to a saint to pray for a person was understandable (if unnecessary). But prayer to a saint to grant something in his own right was out of the question. Particularly inexcusable was the address of prayers to individual saints to whom had been attributed particular functions as patron saints, whether of places or of causes.[6]

Martin Luther shared with Calvin the view that the veneration of saints was in some sense an insult to Jesus Christ, for it took away something of his uniqueness both as intercessor and saviour. In a letter written as early as 1523 to Christians in Latvia and Estonia, he warned them:

> Let no other wind of doctrine move you, whether it blow from Rome or from Jerusalem. Everything depends on faith in Christ and love to one's neighbour. Avoid, as you would deadly poison, indulgences, the worship of saints, and all other works that are applied to ourselves and the good of our souls.[7]

Calvin quotes the fourth-century theologian, Ambrose of Milan, in defence of the central position that should be assigned to Jesus:

> He is our mouth, through which we speak to the Father; he is our eye, through which we see the Father; he is our right hand, through which we offer ourselves to the Father. Unless he intercedes, there is no intercourse with God either for us or for all saints.[8]

So important a principle was at stake here—the uniqueness of trust in Christ—that Luther saw the worship of saints as one of the elements in catholic devotion that it was most important to eliminate. In 1539 George Buchholzer wrote to Luther seeking his advice on whether he should agree to a particular form of church order of which he did not entirely approve. Luther replied that Buchholzer should happily put up with vestments, processions, and the like, provided that the margrave permitted the gospel to be preached with purity and power and 'if he is willing to abolish the invocation of saints (as if they were mediators, intercessors, and deliverers).'[9]

Calvin tries to define in what sense the saints do pray and comes to the conclusion that they are not involved in earthly cares. He is not convinced by the argument that the saints must pray for the living because of the bonds of love within the communion of saints:

> They do not abandon their own repose so as to be drawn into earthly cares; and much less must we on this account be always calling upon them![10]

Their prayer is a sort of yearning for God's kingdom with a set and immovable will. If that really is prayer, then Calvin will say that the saints pray, though as much for the destruction of the wicked as for the salvation of believers, but that is as far as he will go.

It may therefore seem that both the great thinkers of the continental Reformation were entirely negative in their attitude to the saints. This would not be an entirely accurate picture. Luther hailed the evangelical Christians of the Netherlands who had been persecuted, and some martyred, as 'real saints':

> God be praised and blessed for ever that we who have known and worshipped so many false saints have lived to see and hear real saints and true martyrs.[11]

Like Calvin, his quarrel was with false saints and with false honour to saints, not with the idea that some men and women can be held up as special examples of the grace of God at work. The problem came when the blood of the martyrs was seen as winning for their brethren the forgiveness of sins. Calvin quoted Saint Augustine's disapproval of such a view. The virtue of the death of martyrs lies in the fact that they glorify God through their death, they attest to his truth by their blood, and they bear witness by their contempt of the present life to the fact that they are seeking a better life. Calvin thus advanced the protestant view that the saints were to be commemorated for their holy lives in the past and for the example they gave, rather than because of their prayers in the present. In England such a view was to receive recognition in the worship of the Church within a generation.

## ii

The English Reformation in Henry VIII's reign was not identical with what was going on at the same time on the continent. As far as the veneration of saints was concerned, there was perhaps a greater interest in the external signs of such veneration than in the underlying doctrine. Cranmer, Hooper, Jewel, Latimer, and Ridley all wrote of the evils arising from the veneration of images. They had less to say about purgatory and about the prayers of the saints, though they became increasingly vociferous about these after the death of Henry in 1547. Their earlier reticence is explicable in political terms. Henry would not allow doctrinal change to go too far, but he was only too willing to sanction the destruction of shrines if wealth accrued to the crown as a result of such destruction. The Henrician reformers had to be patient.

In 1533 Hugh Latimer, soon to be Bishop of Worcester, was prepared to defend the concept of purgatory. After a sermon in Bristol he had been accused of denying the doctrine. But in clarifying his position, he says that the departed

> have charity in such sure tie that they cannot lose it, so that they cannot murmur nor grudge against God; cannot dishonour God; can neither displease God nor be displeased with God; cannot be dissevered from God; cannot die, nor be in peril of death; cannot be damned, nor be in peril of damnation; cannot but be in surety of salvation. They be members of the mystical body of Christ as we be, and in more surety than we be. They love us charitably. Charity is not idle; if it be, it worketh and sheweth itself: and therefore I say, they wish us well, and pray for us.[12]

In the main this is the orthodox medieval doctrine of purgatory. But there are two novel features. There is a notable absence of reference to suffering, cleansing, and fire. The emphasis is on waiting, and, though later Latimer writes that he did not deny the possibility of pain in purgatory, the cleansing is clearly not for him the major factor. This formulation of the doctrine is also notable for its return to a more primitive idea of reciprocal prayer. He asserts that the dead in purgatory pray for the living, in contradiction of medieval opinion which had lost sight of mutual prayers within the communion of saints.

Latimer's views of purgatory more in terms of waiting is echoed in Archbishop Thomas Cranmer's reply to the west country rebels of 1549. Cranmer preferred to speak of 'paradise', rather than purgatory, and of its characteristics as joy and consolation, rather than pain or torment. Such a view was, for Cranmer, the catholic faith.[13] Its development from the position taken up sixteen years before by Latimer is clear.

The view less sympathetic to any idea of purgatory, however redefined, that Calvin had embraced, was not unknown in England. Myles Coverdale, Bishop of Exeter, who spent many years of exile on the continent, translated in English an anonymous German document entitled *The Defence of a Certain Poor Christian Man who else should have been condemned by the Pope's Law*, which argued strongly against purgatory on scriptural grounds, rejecting one by one the same texts that Calvin had examined in the *Institutes*.[14] Cranmer cannot have been ignorant of these views. That he declined to accept them even after the death of Henry indicated a wish to maintain an independent view. The idea of paradise that he mentioned, the redefined purgatory of which Latimer wrote, has always been distinctive in Anglican thought.

But Latimer's view of mutual prayer was not typical of the English writers of the time, though John Bradford, John Jewel, and Myles Coverdale did all acknowledge that prayer for the dead was in some sense at least permitted in the early Church. Coverdale believed that it was never in the sense of seeking deliverance for the dead. It was rather an expression of solidarity and affection and was therefore more appropriately described as a 'memorial' than as a prayer. And in the practice of the Church of his own day he advocated that, in recalling the dead before God, the language of memorial, rather than of intercession, should be used. He believed that, when a Christian died, the emphasis in funeral rites should be on thanksgiving that the soul was delivered from the miseries of this world.[15]

But what of prayers to the saints? The most systematic exposition of reformed teaching by an English theologian at that time was that by John Hooper, later Bishop of Gloucester and of Worcester, in *A Declaration of Christ and of his Office*, published in 1547. Hooper represented a more extreme protestantism than most of his fellow bishops and only accepted a bishopric when references to saints and angels were removed from his consecration oaths. Hooper, like Calvin, was concerned above all else to restore Jesus Christ to his pre-eminent position as sole mediator between God and man. He wrote:

> This intercession of Christ only sufficeth. No man should seek any other mediator or intercession or expiation of sin, as Paul saith, declaring the sufficiency and ability of Christ's death and intercession.

To invoke the saints is to demote Christ and thus to insult God. Hooper continued:

> What intolerable ill, blasphemy of God, and ethnical idolatry is this, to admit and teach the invocation of saints departed out of this world! It taketh from God his true honour; it maketh him a fool. . . . It diminisheth the merits of Christ.[16]

Coverdale[17] and Latimer[18] echoed such a sentiment, and there is virtual unanimity on this point among the English reformers. Hooper goes on to answer the view that prayer to saints is of a different type to that to God, the view that Christ alone is a mediator in the sense of one who can blot out sins, but the saints are also mediators in the sense that they pray to God. Latimer, for instance, writes:

> As touching the saints in heaven, I said, they be not our mediators by way of redemption; for so Christ alone is our mediator and their both: so that the blood of martyrs hath nothing to do by way of redemption; the blood of Christ is enough for a thousand worlds. But by way of intercession, so saints in heaven may be mediators, and pray for us: as I think they do when we call not upon them; for they be charitable, and need no spurs.[19]

Hooper dismisses this distinction because

> it is the office only of Christ to be the mediator for sin, and likewise to offer the prayers of the Church to his Father . . . As concerning intercession, he commandeth us only to ask in his name, and prescribed the manner how to ask, and what to ask.[20]

So what place is there in Christian life and devotion for the saints of God? Latimer provides an answer in another sermon preached in 1552:

> If thou wilt needs worship them, will you hear how you shall worship them? Live godly and uprightly after their examples; follow their charitable life and steadfast faith; then you worship them as they ought to be worshipped.[21]

As on the continent, so also in England, the Reformation teachers believed that, if there was any virtue in commemorating saints (and men like Hooper saw no such virtue), it was for their example, not their intercession.

## iii

The English reformers knew that they would not change the devotional habits of the people simply by rewriting the liturgy of the Church, though liturgical change was to be part of the process. The ordinary worshipper was probably far more influenced by the visual—the image of the saint, the shrine of the saint, and the pilgrimage to it— than by the theology of the liturgy. There was a good deal of polemical writing against the use of images, not only of course the images of the saints but of Jesus Christ himself. Destroy the image and the shrine, and the ordinary man is forced to change his devotional habits. Both John Jewel[22] and Nicholas Ridley[23] wrote at length about the subject, the latter addressing a plea 'in the name, as it seemeth, of the whole clergy' to Edward VI. There had been a considerable decline in the hundred years or so before the Reformation in pilgrimages and visits to shrines. Their appeal in the Middle Ages had not continued. And, significantly perhaps, the destruction of shrines does not feature as one of the principal complaints of the protest movements, whether in the north or the west country, against other religious reforms. But, if the average Englishman was not as willing as his forefathers to set out for Canterbury, Walsingham, or some more local shrine, he did still attach a good deal of importance to the images of saints that he found in his own local church.

There were arguments in favour of allowing him to continue to do so. Jewel knew what the early theologians of the Church had said:

> St Gregory calleth them the laymen's books; and the fathers in a later council say: 'We may learn more in a short while by an image, than by long study and travail in the scriptures.' And for the same cause St. Basil compareth an image painted with a story written.[24]

John Hooper, never one to understate a case, commented on such a view:

> Oh! blasphemous and devilish doctrine, to appoint the most noble creature of God, man endued with wit and reason, resembling the image of the everlasting God, to be instructed and taught of a mute, dumb, blind, and dead idol![25]

Jewel, in a more restrained way, though he acknowledged that some might indeed learn from images, believed that God intended man to come to a faith in him, not by seeing or gazing, but by hearing. So he rejected the traditional argument. He also did so when he was presented with the suggestion that there was a distinction between the honour given to God and the honour given to the image of a saint, the two types being described as *latria* and *doulia*. *Latria* is the honour given only to God, *doulia*, which may be translated as 'service', given to anything less than God. The distinction, Jewel thought, was a false one and relied in any case on the ordinary people being sufficiently well informed to know the distinction and abide by it. Whether *latria* or *doulia*, idolatry was the likely outcome.[26]

Archbishop Cranmer made a different distinction, that between seeing an image and worshipping it. Presumably he thought that ordinary people could recognise this distinction. In *c.* 1538 (and therefore while Henry VIII still exercised influence over religious reform) he wrote:

Although all images, be they engraven, painted, or wrought in arras, or in any otherwise made, be so prohibited that they may neither be bowed down unto nor worshipped (forasmuch as they be the works of man's hands only), yet be they not so prohibited, but they may be had and set up in churches, so it be for none other purpose but only to the intent that we (in beholding and looking upon them, as in certain books, and seeing represented in them the manifold examples of virtues, which were in saints, represented by the said images) may the rather be provoked, kindled, and stirred to yield thanks to our Lord and praise him in his said saints.[27]

Such a distinction Hooper regarded as 'childish.'[28] Cranmer himself did not see it as a justification for shrines or pilgrimages, for only a few years later he issued repeated instructions for the removal of shrines and all that went with them. And later still he joined in the attack on images.[29]

Bishop Latimer examined yet another distinction, or rather a distinction quite beyond the ordinary people who therefore confused 'images of saints' and 'inhabiters of heaven', both of whom they called 'saints'. Though the inhabiters of heaven may be prayed to, dead images may not. Thus, although Latimer believed that the saints in heaven can be mediators by praying for the living, he has to say of images:

There be two manner of mediators, one by way of redemption, another by way of intercession; and I said, that these saints, that is to say, images called saints, be mediators neither way.[30]

It is not surprising, therefore, with all these subtle confusions and distinctions, that the English reformers came to see the only possible solution in the widespread, if not complete, removal of images. Jewel believed the abolition of images to be the only real answer.[31] Cranmer, though he did not go so far, repeatedly sought to remove all objects of veneration.[32] Ridley, Bishop of London, linking the alleged abuse with several others, issued an instruction to his diocese in 1550:

That none maintain purgatory, invocation of saints, the six articles, beadrolls, images, reliques, rubrick primars, with invocation of saints, justification of man by his own works, . . . or any other such like abuses and superstitions, now taken away by the king's grace's most godly proceedings.[33]

But, despite such instructions issued throughout the land, the medieval tradition died very slowly. Saints continued to be invoked, even where the shrines or the images had gone.

Pilgrimages were made to the famous well of St. Winifred at Holywell throughout the seventeenth century. John Aubrey records the story of a parish clerk in Wiltshire, appointed under Mary Tudor but still in office in the reign of James I, who at the end of his life still

> when the gad-fly had happened to sting his oxen, or cows, and made them run away in that champaign country, he would run after them, crying out, praying, 'Good Saint Katherine of Winterbourne, stay my oxen.'[34]

Cranmer was already discovering the difficulties of rooting out such time-honoured practices when in 1548 he wrote one of his instructions for the removal of images. Some men were

> being so superstitious, or rather wilful, as they would by their good wills retain all such images still, although they have been most manifestly abused; and in some places also the images which by the said injunctions were taken down be now restored and set up again.[35]

The reformers were faced with a difficult task. But the destruction of shrines and images was not their only way forward. They could incorporate new doctrine in the liturgy of the Church and in the law of the land.

## iv

Change was gradual and at first invocation of the saints as intercessors was maintained. The 'Articles about Religion set forth by the Convocation and published by the King's authority', usually known as the 'Ten Articles', of 1536 instructed bishops and preachers to teach the people to honour the saints, though not with the honour due only to God, taking the saints to be the 'advancers of our prayers and demands' to Christ. A model form of prayer to the saints was provided:

> All holy angels and saints in Heaven pray for us and with us unto the Father, that for his dear Son Jesus Christ's sake we may have grace of him, and remission of our sins.[36]

The 'Bishops' Book' of the following year and the 'King's Book' of 1543 commended the same practice, but warned against improper forms of prayer asking the saints for gifts that come from God alone. This position, developed in successive documents of Henry's reign, was in substantial agreement with that taken up by the Roman Catholic Church as it restated its doctrine at the Council of Trent. The Council decreed:

> The saints reigning together with Christ offer their prayers to God on behalf of men, and it is good and useful to invoke them as suppliants and to take refuge in their prayers, support, and help, on account of the benefits to be obtained from God through this from Jesus Christ our Lord. . . . All superstition in the invocation of saints is to be put down.[37]

With the death of Henry came a change in emphasis. The First Prayer Book in 1549 commemorated the saints and the departed in general in these words:

> And here we do give unto thee most high praise, and hearty thanks, for the wonderful grace and virtue, declared in all thy saints, from the beginning of the world: and chiefly in the glorious and most blessed virgin Mary, mother of thy son Jesus Christ our Lord and God, and in the holy Patriarchs, Prophets, Apostles and Martyrs, whose examples, O Lord, and steadfastness in thy faith, and keeping thy holy commandments, grant us to follow. We commend unto thy mercy, O Lord, all other thy servants, which are departed hence from us, with the sign of faith, and now do rest in the sleep of peace: Grant unto them, we beseech thee, thy mercy, and everlasting peace, and that, at the day of the general resurrection, we and all they which be of the mystical body of thy son, may altogether be set on his right hand . . .[38]

The saints are here commemorated in a spirit of thankfulness for their example. The departed in general are prayed for by the living. But there is no invocation of saints. This whole section was omitted in the revision of 1552. The Prayer for the Church in the Eucharist in 1552 stops short after prayer for the sick and suffering and the departed are not commemorated at all.[39] The attitude of that book to the departed emerges in the Burial rite where thanks is given to God that he has delivered the soul of the departed person from this sinful world and God is asked

> shortly to accomplish the number of thine elect, and to hasten thy kingdom, that we with this our brother, and all others departed in the true faith of thy holy name, may have our perfect consummation and bliss, both in body and soul, in thy eternal and everlasting glory.[40]

In this book not only is all reference to the saints, even thankfulness for their example, omitted, but no prayer is made for the dead, whose fate is considered sealed at the hour of death.

The 'Forty-two Articles' of the following year made it clear why the saints had been omitted. Issued by the bishops, they dismissed the invocation of saints as 'a fond thing vainly feigned'. Or, to be more exact, they dismissed 'the doctrine of school authors concerning . . . the invocation of saints'. What precisely they meant by that has been the subject of a good deal of debate. When the articles were reissued in Elizabeth's reign, 'the doctrine of school authors' had been changed to 'the Romish doctrine', an equally ambiguous phrase. What precisely was being condemned?[41] The most obvious answer is that the whole doctrine as it had developed from the beginning was implied. Examination of the views of both continental and English reformers has already suggested that such condemnation was seen by the majority of them as natural and even necessary.[42] But why specify 'the doctrine of school authors' or 'the Romish doctrine'? There have always been those who have argued that this wording implies a criticism only of Roman abuses, such as prayer to images, prayer to grant more than simply the gift of intercession. They have suggested that 'the Romish doctrine' was 'an expression used in the sixteenth century to denote the [teaching of the] extreme medieval party in the Church.'[43]

It is impossible to be sure which interpretation is right. But what is certain is that invocation of saints has never since featured in Anglican liturgy in England. Whatever the articles originally intended, they soon came to be taken as a complete condemnation of all prayer to the saints or with the saints. By removing entirely from the service books any kind of invocation and by drawing up articles that condemned at very least the extreme practices and ways of thought in which saints had been called upon, the reformers made it unlikely that invocation would survive, even if, according to one interpretation, they left it an open question whether the clergy might express approval of the practice of invocation of saints in the limited sense of seeking from the saints the help of their prayers. Such approval could not be enshrined in the liturgy.

## V

Although the saints were to receive no mention in the liturgy until 1662 (and even then in only a very restrained way), their memory was preserved in place names and in church dedications, there being no serious attempt to destroy these. Unique among reformed churches, the Church of England under Cranmer and again in Elizabeth's reign preserved a calendar of the saints and required that some of the saints be commemorated by a special collect and readings.

Cranmer had a particular interest in this subject and several of his attempts to produce an ideal calendar survive. In the pre-Reformation Church, the Roman calendar had been supplemented, not only in every country by national saints, but in particular churches and cathedrals by saints of local or special interest. In England, since the development of printing, the Sarum calendar had become widely used, but these local variations still continued. In Cranmer's own cathedral city, Canterbury, a different calendar was in use in the cathedral and in St. Augustine's abbey. Early Roman saints and English saints of every age were strongly represented in these calendars, which were made the more complicated by the observance of 'octaves' (the eighth day of a feast, given almost as much dignity as the feast itself). Cranmer was clearly right to set about a revision and simplification. In Henry's reign the only changes were to strike out the feast of St. Thomas Becket and to rename any 'pope' who appeared in the calendar 'bishop of Rome', both alterations being made for obvious political reasons.

Cranmer has left behind two draft calendars.[44] The principal features of the first were a reduction of the total number of holy days, the omission of octaves, a preponderance of New Testament saints and eastern saints, and a lack of English saints. Cranmer's second draft included nearly all the names in the first, but in addition there was a richer provision of English saints (such as Edward the martyr, Augustine, and Alban) and also an enormous importation of sixty heroes of the Old Testament and the Apocrypha. This was enthusiasm for holy Scripture carried to excess. Though patriarchs and prophets had been named in various medieval litanies and calendars, there had never been anything on this scale before. And indeed Cranmer himself thought better of the matter and these Old Testament figures did not feature in the calendar of the Prayer Book of 1549.

The sort of change that the calendar was undergoing can best be seen by examining in some detail the provision made at different times for the first fifteen days of the year (set out on p. 58). Cranmer's starting point was the Sarum calendar. In his own draft he omitted from Sarum all provision in the first half of

| | *Pre-Reformation Sarum Calendar*[45] | *Pre-Reformation Calendar Christ Church Canterbury* | *Cranmer's second draft* | *Book of Common Prayer 1549 and 1552* | *Primer 1553* | *Calendar 1559* |
|---|---|---|---|---|---|---|
| 1 | Circumcision | Circumcision | Circumcision | Circumcision | Circumcision | Circumcision |
| 2 | Octave of Stephen | | Abel | | | |
| 3 | Octave of John | Genevieve | Noah | | | |
| 4 | Octave of the Innocents | | Titus | | | |
| 5 | Octave of Thomas Becket | | | | | |
| 6 | Epiphany | Epiphany | Epiphany | Epiphany | Epiphany | Epiphany |
| 7 | | Abraham | | | | |
| 8 | Lucian | | Lucian | | Lucian | Lucian |
| 9 | | Adrian | Sara | | | |
| 10 | | Paul Hermit | | | | |
| 11 | | | | | | |
| 12 | | | | | | |
| 13 | Octave of Epiphany; Hilary | Octave of Epiphany; Hilary | Hilary | | Hilary | Hilary |
| 14 | Felix | Felix | Felix; Isaac | | Felix | |
| 15 | Maurus | Maurus | Jacob | | Maurus | |

January of octave days for St. Stephen, St. John, the Innocents, St. Thomas Becket (already removed by Henry), and the Epiphany. He was content to retain not only the major feasts, the Circumcision and the Epiphany, but also the feasts of lesser saints—St. Lucian, an obscure priest-martyr of Beauvais about whom nothing is known for certain, St. Hilary, the great fourth-century Bishop of Poitiers and fierce opponent of Arianism, and St. Felix of Nola[46]. Only St. Maurus, a sixth-century monk, allegedly brought up by St. Benedict, lost his place. There was only one new name in Cranmer's first draft of these dates, that of St. Titus, a New Testament figure, reputedly bishop in Crete, commemorated on 4 January. In his second draft appeared Abel, Noah, Abraham, Sara, Isaac (who shared a day with Felix of Nola), and Jacob, all old Testament figures. Cranmer's intention was to commemorate these heroes, and also the Christian saints, by reading on their feast a short biography of them. He began to write (in Latin) such biographies, but abandoned the task.[47]

The Prayer Books of 1549 and 1552 reflected wise second thoughts by Cranmer. Gone were all the strange innovations. But gone also were nearly all the minor saints days. The major feasts were reduced in number in 1549 by the omission of, for instance, the Assumption and the Conception of Mary, and in that first book there were no minor feasts. The 1552 book retained the major feasts of 1549 except that St. Mary Magdalen was omitted. Four minor feasts were reintroduced—St. George, St. Laurence, St. Clement, and Lammas Day. Why these four in particular it is impossible to know. The way that they were introduced was however quite significant. For they were listed in the calendar, yet no liturgical provision was made for them. There was no indication at all in the rubrics as to how they were to be observed.

The introduction of a book to be used throughout the land meant the end of the individual calendars in use in particular churches. The Sarum order had gradually established itself in most places, but great monasteries and cathedrals retained their own independent calendars. Christ Church Cathedral in Canterbury in its calendar included, in the early days of January, Hilary, Felix, and Maurus, though not Lucian. In addition it named St. Genevieve, the fifth-century patron saint of Paris, and St. Paul of Thebes, venerated as the first Christian hermit. These omissions from Cranmer's calendar were not of great significance. But a third omission, that of St. Adrian, was. Adrian was an

African who accompanied St. Theodore to Canterbury, became abbot there, and contributed much to the life of the Church of his time, particularly by building up Christian education in Canterbury itself. He was not a saint of universal importance, but his significance for Canterbury is clear and it was an impoverishment of the English calendar that local observances were removed. Had Cranmer's plan to include Old Testament heroes not been abandoned, the canons of Canterbury would have found themselves commemorating on 9 January not Adrian, a local figure of less than a thousand years before, but Sara, wife of Abraham, a legendary figure of the very distant past.

The Primer of 1553, 'a book of private prayer needful to be used of all Christians', authorised by Edward VI, marks a return to a more traditional calendar.[48] It follows very closely the 1552 Prayer Book in its theology and its language. It comes therefore as something of a surprise to find that the calendar is almost exactly that of the Sarum order, but with octave days and feasts of such politically controversial saints as Thomas Becket omitted. The provision for the first fifteen days of January is exactly that of Sarum with the octaves omitted. Lucian, Hilary, Felix, and even Maurus have all returned, although, as with the few minor saints' days in 1552, there is no suggestion as to how they should be observed.

The five years that followed saw the temporary undoing of Cranmer's work and also his own death, together with the death of most of those (Hooper, Latimer, and Ridley among them) who had challenged the medieval view of saints. But, in 1559, Elizabeth's Prayer Book was almost exactly that of 1552. Its calendar was identical. Two years later a commission headed by Matthew Parker, the Archbishop of Canterbury, was appointed to consider the calendar. The result of its deliberations was a calendar almost identical with that contained in the Book of Common Prayer of 1662 as in use today. Of the saints of 1662, only Charles I, Bede, Alban, and Enurchus were not included in Parker's proposals. The calendar was based on that of Sarum, but the criteria used in making the selection are not entirely clear.[49] Among the minor feasts, there are fifty-four saints. Four are biblical and a fifth, Anne, the mother of Mary, belongs to the New Testament period. Only thirteen, less than a quarter, are British saints. David represents the sixth century, Augustine, Etheldreda, and Chad the seventh, Boniface the eighth, Edmund of East Anglia and Swithun the ninth, Dunstan and Edward of the West Saxons (commemorated twice) the tenth, Alphege and Edward the Confessor the eleventh, and Hugh and Richard the thirteenth. Prominent among the omissions were Aidan, Alban (added in 1662), Anselm, Bede (added in 1662), Columba, Cuthbert, Hilda, and Patrick. Of the foreign saints, twenty-two were martyrs, most of them of the early centuries and of Rome. Five (Ambrose, Augustine of Hippo, Gregory, Hilary, and Jerome) were great theologians, all of them giants of the western church. But the churches of the east, that could have been represented by John Chrysostom, Basil, or many more, received no representation. The remaining nine were a strange collection of bishops and abbots. Benedict and Martin (commemorated twice) would earn a place in any calendar. The places of Brice, Leonard, and Machutus are more difficult to justify. It was an odd compilation. But its impact upon English worship was in any case very limited because of the fact that until 1928 there was to be no official provision of collects for these minor saints' days and so they went almost entirely unobserved. Only with a great interest in the saints in the nineteenth century was this calendar seen to be lacking in balance and unhelpful in worship.

Cranmer's has been the most important influence on the compiling of Anglican calendars and material to commemorate saints. It has meant, for instance, that obscure biblical figures rank above even the greatest of Christian heroes of later ages. Jude or Matthias, because they were apostles, are commemorated with collect and readings, a 'red-letter' feast. Augustine or Athanasius, two of the most significant theologians of the Christian Church, are named in the calendar but not in the liturgy, a 'black-letter' feast. National and local festivals are not encouraged. It is a biblical approach and one that exalts the apostolic churches at the expense of the succeeding Christian centuries. Subsequent Anglican revision has not seriously challenged this view.

# 5 *The Anglican Way*

i

Although Cranmer and the sixteenth century gave Anglicanism its liturgy, it is to a later period that Anglicans have traditionally turned to find the classic expression of distinctive Anglican theology. The nineteenth century, especially, looked back with particular respect to the so-called 'Caroline divines' and, although by these were usually meant a particular sort of 'high-churchman', it is certainly the seventeenth century that provides the most creative period of distinctive Anglican theology, save perhaps for the early years of the twentieth century.

Richard Baxter, anything but a high-churchman, wrote in 1647, when he mistakenly thought himself to be on his death bed, a work entitled *The Saints' Everlasting Rest.*[1] It is a devotional work rather than a doctrinal one, but one of great theological insight. One of its most interesting features is that it fails to face the question of the moment when the departed are admitted to the joys of heaven, joys which it describes in a compelling and poetic way. To read what he wrote in *The Saints' Everlasting Rest* would be to gain the impression that these joys were waiting just the other side of death. Yet Baxter, like Anglicans of every generation since the Reformation, have had their view of after-life moulded by a burial rite which asks God

> that it may please thee, of thy gracious goodness, shortly to accomplish the number of thine elect, and to hasten thy kingdom; that we, with all those that are departed in the true faith of thy holy name, may have our perfect consummation and bliss . . .

Baxter shows an important Anglican characteristic in totally ignoring this perspective in the Church's teaching. The Last Judgement and the general resurrection at the end of time seem to make less impact on him than the moment of death which is apparently, for him, the moment of decision—God's decision—and he does not speak in terms of any intermediate state. Once dead, the enjoyment of God or the loss of God is the immediate choice:

> When we have obtained the haven, we have done sailing. When the workman hath his wages, it is implied he hath done his work. When we are at our journey's end, we have done with the way. All motion ends at the centre, and all means cease when we have the end.

This emphasis of death as the time of judgement was strong in seventeenth-century thinking, whatever the Burial Service might say. Thomas Morton, Bishop of Durham until 1659, attacked what he called the Romish doctrine because the Scripture

> assureth the Church that all such as die in Christ are in blessed rest from their labours, but the wicked and such as die in their sins sink down to the lowest hell.[2]

Purgatory was not really an issue of great consequence in the seventeenth century, though Archbishop William Wake wrote a systematic attack on it published in 1687.[3] But if that century presented a united viewpoint on purgatory, it did not do so on prayer for the departed. Bishop Morton, believing that the wicked are consigned to hell at death, regarded prayer for them as hopeless. No Roman Catholic would have disputed that. In fact Joseph Hall, Bishop of Norwich, quotes Cardinal Bellarmine as saying that prayers 'profit neither the blessed nor the damned souls; the former need them not, the latter cannot be aided by them.'[4] Bellarmine believed in prayer only for those neither blessed nor damned, in other words those in purgatory. Since Bishop Hall did not believe in purgatory, he did not believe in prayer for the dead. Prayer for the living was a far more healthy activity! William Nicholl, in a very balanced argument,[5] noted that the Church of England had not condemned prayer for the dead, but nor had it sanctioned it. Men were at liberty to hold it as a private theological opinion, but it was difficult to maintain that the Church encouraged something which men were not authorised to preach and had no warrant in the Bible or in the service books of the Church, 'which is so far from recommending it, that for 150 years she has plainly discountenanced it.'

But, against this opinion can be drawn up a formidable line of theologians, not least Lancelot Andrewes, Bishop of Winchester, whose *Preces Privatae* have formed so important a part of Anglican devotional literature. One of the prayers in that work includes these words:

Give to the living mercy and grace,
to the dead rest and light perpetual;
give to the Church truth and peace,
to us sinners penitence and pardon.[6]

How then did Andrewes, and those who prayed in a similar fashion, justify such prayer? The defenders of the practice were united, first of all, in their claim that praying for the dead need not for one moment imply a belief in purgatory. Jeremy Taylor[7] and John Bramhall,[8] both bishops of Irish sees, made this point most emphatically. Their appeal was to the antiquity of the practice. Praying for the dead was the practice of the Church long before ideas of purgatory developed. Indeed there is more than a hint in the writings of several theologians of dissatisfaction at the poor provision of prayer for the dead in the Anglican liturgy. William Forbes, Bishop of Edinburgh, expressed it thus:

> Would to God, that the Church of England . . . had in this matter and in a few others rather conformed herself to the most ancient custom of the universal Church, than on account of the errors and abuses which little by little crept in afterwards, absolutely to have rejected and entirely to have abolished it, to the great scandal of almost all other Christians.[9]

But it is Archbishop Bramhall who, in giving his justification of prayer for the dead despite lack of belief in purgatory, comes nearest to providing a theological position that holds together the two differing emphases that place the moment of judgement at death and at the end of the world. He writes:

> Though the sins of the faithful be privately and particularly remitted at the day of death, yet the public promulgation of their pardon at the Day of Judgement is to come. Though their souls be always in an estate of blessedness, yet they want the consummation of this blessedness, extensively at least, until the body be reunited with the soul; and (as it is piously and probably believed) intensively also,— that the soul hath not yet so full and clear a vision of God, as it shall have hereafter.

He holds the two emphases in tension very cleverly. But, however much the seventeenth century rejected the name 'purgatory', he is quite prepared to defend the intermediate state, provided that it is a state characterised not by purging, but by waiting. And, although it is impossible to detect a view held sufficiently widespread to be called 'the seventeenth-century position', there does seem to have been virtual agreement among the seventeenth-century theologians whose opinions subsequent ages have respected—Andrewes, Taylor, Thorndike, as well as Bramhall—that the dead who are to be saved, yet await the final judgement, can benefit from the prayers of the living, in accordance with the practice of the very early Church, however inadequate the expression of such belief in Anglican liturgy.

But there is no such agreement in the seventeenth century on the prayer that the Christian dead offer on behalf of the living and, particularly, on whether the living may reasonably seek such prayers. The balance is probably against the invocation of saints, since, for different reasons, John Bramhall, John Cosin, Richard Hooker, and Jeremy Taylor all oppose the practice. The first objection, almost inevitably, is the lack of scriptural warrant. This is Hooker's objection[10] and it is shared by Bramhall, who writes:

> We have no command from God to invocate them . . . but we have another command, 'Call upon me in the day of trouble, and I will hear thee'. We have no promise to be heard, when we do invocate them; but we have another promise,—'Whatsoever ye shall ask the Father in My name, ye shall receive it.' We have no example in Holy Scripture of any that did invocate them, but rather the contrary: 'See thou do it not'; 'I am thy fellow servant, worship God.'[11]

Bramhall goes on to throw doubt on whether the saints are in possession of the necessary information to pray for us. How aware of our condition they are can only be a matter of conjecture. Like Bishop Hall[12], he believes that to pray to a saint must mean that the saint possesses insight which only God can have. It therefore makes the saint into a deity. But Bishop Forbes thinks this unnecessarily cautious. He recalls that the early Christian theologians of the patristic age sought the prayers of the saints in heaven and justifies the practice thus:

> For although it be altogether uncertain whether they have an *idiopatheia* (to use the expression of some Protestants), that is, a particular acquaintance with our necessities and distresses, yet who in their senses would deny to them a *sympatheia* or general knowledge derived from the Word of God and their own past experience?[13]

Jeremy Taylor[14] shares the view that we cannot know whether the saints hear our prayers. Indeed not only that, we do not really know who they are, let alone where they are. But Thomas Ken, the non-juring Bishop of Bath and Wells, not only thought he knew that the saints prayed for us, but felt able to define a saint in a very wide sense, for at the funeral of Lady Margaret Mainard, no doubt a worthy soul but no 'saint' in a technical sense, he said in his sermon:

> We were all travelling the same way, as pilgrims towards our heavenly country. She has only got the start of us, and is gone before, and is happy first, and I am persuaded that we shall still enjoy her prayers for us above.[15]

This is precisely the mutual and reciprocal prayer practiced in the early Church but which it has been so difficult to detect in later ages. The belief is implicit in what Herbert Thorndike, a prebendary of Westminster, wrote when he spoke of

> the prayers, which those that depart in the highest favour with God make for us, (and in) the prayers which we make for those that depart in the lowest degree of favour with God.[16]

It is Thorndike who produces the most systematic exposition of invocation[17] in his time. He distinguishes three sorts of prayer to saints. The first is prayer to God asking for his blessings by and through the merits and intercession of the saints. It is quite clear to Thorndike that prayers along those lines are perfectly acceptable. The second is prayer addressed to the saint but in the form '*Ora pro nobis*', 'Pray for us', or '*Te rogamus audi nos*', 'We beseech thee to hear us'. And these he regards as controversial and writes a good deal about them. The third sort is when the saint is asked to grant requests that only God can grant. And such are idolatrous and Thorndike dismisses and condemns them outright. But of the *Ora pro nobis* sort, he is less certain. He knows that such prayer was offered in the days of the fathers and recognises that it cannot be called idolatry. Nevertheless the consequence of it can be indistinguishable from idolatry and the Church is therefore well advised to avoid such usage. Thorndike therefore comes out in favour of prayer to God asking for the help of the saints, but against seeking that help by direct prayer to them. By implication, therefore, he believes in the prayers of the saints, while believing it unnecessary to present requests for such prayer. He would not have agreed with those who found it impossible to believe that the saints have intimate knowledge of our day-to-day existence. Whether he would have gone as far as Bishop Montague of Norwich it is impossible to know. Montague agreed that Christians on earth should not pray to the saints *Ora pro nobis.* Nevertheless he was quite willing to believe that some Saint or Saints departed may have more special care of, interest in, charge over, some men or man, country or countries, than is used ordinarily . . . Examples hereof are frequent and many:— St. George is accounted the Patron of England; Saint Andrew of Scotland; Saint James for Spain; others for other peoples and countries anciently chosen and deputed. It needs not be tendered or held as *de fide.* It is no point of necessity to salvation. It may be true. There is no impiety in believing so or so. Nor doth this opinion of a general protection infer any special intercession. This I am sure, the ancients supposed it, and were of opinion, yet never said to any such patron saint, *Ora pro nobis* or *pro me.*[18]

The view that has emerged from the seventeenth century is therefore a diverse one. There is a good deal more agnosticism about the state of the dead and the validity of prayers to and by them than could be detected in previous centuries. There is a good deal more sympathy to a catholic, if not a 'Romish' (if the distinction is valid), viewpoint, especially is there a willingness to recognise that a case had been made out for prayer between living and dead by some of the theologians of the patristic age. In their general tone, the views expressed, whether they favour invocation of saints or not, are far more sympathetic to the idea of saints and far more inclined to honour them than the expressions of opinion of the previous century. Let the final words belong to Bishop Hall of Norwich, for they sum up what was probably the majority opinion:

O ye blessed saints above, we honour your memories as far as we ought; we do with praise recount your virtues; we magnify your victories; we bless God, for your happy exemption from the misery of this world, and for your estating in that blessed immortality; we imitate your holy examples; we long and pray for a happy consociation with you. We dare not raise temples, dedicate altars, direct prayers to you; we dare not, finally, offer any thing to you which you are unwilling to receive, not put anything upon you which you would disclaim as prejudicial to your Creator and Redeemer.[19]

## ii

The eighteenth century has become a much neglected period of Anglican church history, except for study of the Evangelical movements in the latter part of the century. It was by no means a period of such dull inactivity as some have imagined. Nevertheless there were few new insights to the problems that we are considering. The more protestant of the views that we found in the previous century held sway. Not so in the nineteenth century, when the Oxford Movement brought the matter to the fore again. It was inevitable that it should be so, for the leading figures of the Oxford Movement were thought to be 'Romanisers' and that very word itself was a reminder of the article which spoke of 'Romish doctrine concerning purgatory, pardons, worshipping and adoration, as well of images as of relics, and also invocation of saints'. It was brought to the fore also because the Oxford Movement men laid new emphasis on the Eucharist, and any thoughtful eucharistic theology had to lead to a renewed interest in the Church 'triumphant' to which the church militant seemed specially close when it celebrated the Eucharist. Be that as it may, the Oxford Movement theologians were not on the whole creative thinkers, though devious thinkers they certainly were when it came to interpreting Calvinist articles in a catholic light! Their concern was a return to antiquity and this found expression in a profound reverence for the early fathers, especially as these had been represented and interpreted by the seventeenth century divines. Inevitably these Tractarians were as selective as any group about the way they used the writers of the ages to which they looked back with special reverence. Contradictions in the writings of the early Church escape them and, conveniently, only the seventeenth-century writers more sympathetic to 'catholic' ideas seem to come to their notice.

The Tractarian view of the subjects under consideration comes chiefly from two sources. The more famous is John Henry Newman's *Tract XC*, published in 1841 with an Introduction by Edward Pusey, on the Thirty-nine Articles and how they may be interpreted in a catholic sense. Less well known, but more thorough, is a letter of Pusey's published in the same year under the title of *The Articles treated in Tract XC.*[20] Both Newman and Pusey sought to emphasise that what stands condemned in Anglican eyes is only the 'Romish doctrine'. Other doctrines of purgatory or the invocation of saints are not ruled out by the article. In particular the teaching of the early Church is not condemned except insofar as it may coincide with the Romish doctrine. For the early Church had not emphasised suffering and punishment in purgatory in the way that later Roman theologians had done. Pusey wrote:

> If any of the Fathers definitely hold that there will be suffering after this life, for some who shall be saved, it is not an abiding *state* of suffering; and again it is spoken of, solely with respect to the future, as the purifying for the Presence of the All-holy God, not as a 'satisfaction' for past sin, which 'God requires'.

Tertullian, Cyprian, and Augustine are all quoted in support of this view. The early theologians do allow that there will be a fire. Newman describes it thus:

> The conflagration of the world, or the flames which attend the Judge, will be an ordeal through which all men will pass; great saints, such as St. Mary, will pass it unharmed; others will suffer loss; but none will fail under it who are built upon the right foundation. Here is one (doctrine of purgatory) not 'Romish'.

Because it is not 'Romish', it may be held by an Anglican as a matter of private belief. And the same may be said of the Greek emphasis on a *poena damni,* rather than a *poena sensus,* not a positive infliction, let alone the torment of fire, but the absence of God's presence. So too a doctrine that sees the cleansing as a progressive sanctification, involving no pain at all. Nor in fact is the Roman position, as defined at the Council of Trent, intended, for the article was drawn up before the council, and at Trent the Roman Church adopted a very different sort of position to the medieval one, for on purgatory it said (the italics are Newman's):

> Among the uneducated vulgar let *difficult and subtle questions,* which make not for edification, and seldom contribute aught towards piety, be kept back from popular discourses. Neither let them suffer the public mention and treatment of *uncertain points,* or such as *look like falsehood.*[21]

All that stands condemned is the Roman doctrine current in the sixteenth century before Trent and this is, basically, the medieval doctrine.

The same sort of approach that Newman and Pusey used in their defence of non-Romish purgatory applied when they turned to non-Romish teaching on prayer for the dead. What had been condemned, Newman believed, was not prayer for the dead in any form, but prayer offered 'to rescue the lost from eternal fire'. Other prayer was 'lawful', in the sense both that the Church had from the beginning permitted it and also that the law of the Anglican Church allowed it. But not only was it legal. It was 'an unspeakable privilege', at least for Pusey, who saw it as implicit in a doctrine of the Communion of Saints

> that they, in the attainment of certain salvation . . . , shall pray and long for us who are still on the stormy sea of this world, our salvation still unsecured: and that we, on our side, should pray for such things, as God in his goodness wills to bestow on them.

Pusey made much of the word 'love' in the relationship between living and dead. In a striking sentence, he goes on:

> So would God perpetuate divine love beyond the grave; so would he, in the communion of the saints, provide that 'they without us, should not be made perfect', that they who have attained, should be yet indebted to our love, while we are yet more indebted to their love.

These are attractive sentiments. Pusey seemed to have recaptured the sense of loving closeness to the saints that had characterised those friends of the martyred Polycarp seventeen hundred years before.[22] Although Pusey based his argument on patristic theology, it was really an emotional need that he was articulating, that natural desire to pray for those departed to whom he had been close in this life.

In examining earlier periods of history, it had proved possible to examine first the prayers of the Christian living for the Christian dead and, only having done that, to pass on to the prayers of the Christian dead for the Christian living. But already this is proving impossible with the Tractarians who have a greater sense of the mutual interdependence of the two than the majority of either the sixteenth-century reformers or the seventeenth-century theologians in any way sympathetic to the subject. The reciprocity that marks Pusey's words (above) is no isolated example, but occurs repeatedly. John Keble's words are worth quoting at length. They are part of a meditation for All Saints' Day.

> . . . . We have fellowship with one another; fellowship, not only with those now living, but with those who are gone before; and with those who are yet behind, with us. The dead in Christ live; they live unto God; they think of us; they pray for us. Consider how near we must be to each other, when the dead are said to be imperfect without us. A truth in unison with what we read of Christ Himself. 'The Lord hath need of them.' 'The Church which is his Body, the fullness of Him that filleth all in all.' All are imperfect until Christ shall come. Even the best are so, till the Resurrection. And this is true of the Christian saints; the ancient liturgies preserve the tokens of this doctrine; the very highest of the saints used to be named in them; Christ interceding, both for them and for us, in Heaven.[23]

This of course is not the 'Romish doctrine'. The Tractarians drew on a carefully documented objection to the Roman view of invocation by James Ussher, seventeenth-century Archbishop of Armagh. The differences which Ussher had noted between the practice of the early Church and the later Roman Church had been these. In the early Church 'mental addresses' were confined to God, but in the later Roman Church they are also made to saints. The early Church remained agnostic about whether the saints can know the details of our needs, but in the Roman Church it is a matter of faith that they can. In the early Church the dead were addressed just as the living, but in the Roman Church 'formal and absolute' prayers are offered to them. In the early church their aid is sought as co-petitioners to God, but in the Roman Church they are advocates and mediators on account of their merits. In the early Church, fellowship with saints never obscured direct access to God, but in the Roman Church it is often seen as an easier and more acceptable way through to him. In the early Church Christians relied chiefly on their own prayers, in the Roman Church on the prayers of the saints. Pusey, quoting Ussher, concludes:

> 'And principally,' in the Ancient Church, the prayers of the saints were requested as fellow-servants; in the Romish, 'invocation is attributed as a part of the worship due to them, in Bellarmine's words "an eminent kind of adoration".'

Pusey, like Ussher, believed this to be a very important point, because it dictated the sort of frame of mind in which the Christian approached his prayer to the saints. For what is significant is often not so much what people say, but the atmosphere in which it is said. If saints are regarded as semi-divine beings to whom worship is due, words, that if addressed to fellow humans would be quite straight forward, acquire a sinister depth. The objection is to making prayer to the saints part of a systematic devotion, which changes a momentary feeling into habitual devotion. When the prayers take on this tendency, the mind of the worshipper is directed to the saints, rather than through them to God. That was a danger Pusey thought worth underlining heavily. Such devotion, wrong in itself, led almost inevitably to the sort of superstition in which prayers to the saints as fellow-workers became, not only prayer for necessities that only God can grant, but also prayers to particular patrons, prayers that amounted to falling down in worship and offering sacrifices to them. And that, Newman noted, was not only contrary to primitive and Anglican practice, but to that decreed by the Council of Trent.

To the witness of the early Church, the Reformation documents, and the decrees of Trent, Newman (quoting Lancelot Andrewes) and Pusey (quoting Herbert Thorndike's views already set out[24]) add that of the seventeenth century to prove both what the 'Romish' doctrine is and how right the Anglican church was to reject it. But the Tractarians were not entirely united in their view as to what was permissible. Pusey, in quoting Thorndike approvingly, commits himself to a view that the *Ora pro nobis* sort of prayer however inadvisable is nevertheless permissible, if used with great caution. But Keble declares categorically that the living are not to ask the saints to pray for them. Nevertheless for both Pusey and Keble the normal prayer is prayer to God to grant to the living the intercession of the saints. Keble wrote:

> We may have this comfortable thought, that they do remember us. And we may ask this petition of God, that the prayers of the saints being offered for the Church, may be effectual for our personal good.[25]

## iii

Osmund, the eleventh-century Bishop of Salisbury, was canonised in 1457 and he was the last Englishman to be made a saint by the pope before the Reformation. Repeated attempts were made to secure the canonisation of King Henry VI and there was a considerable veneration of him in some political (rather than strictly religious) circles in England at the end of the fifteenth century.[26] When Archbishop Cranmer was at work on his revisions of the calendar,[27] he did not give any weight to the idea (if indeed it occured to him) of including any of the Christian figures who had devoted their lives to the defence of the sort of views for which he himself stood. William Tyndale, for instance, had been martyred for the Protestant cause in 1536 and, nearly two hundred years before, John Wyclif had made the sort of protest against the papacy that had now spread across Europe and become fashionable in England. Cranmer did not however include them. The Elizabethan revisers of the calendar similarly did not include the martyrs of the previous reign—Hugh

Latimer, Nicholas Ridley, and Thomas Cranmer himself preeminent among them. Perhaps their deaths were too much part of the present, rather than of history. Perhaps it would have been politically inept—almost certainly so. Or perhaps the English church felt uncertain about how to proceed with canonisation now that papal authority was gone. Certainly, whatever the reason, the Elizabethan calendar included no saint later than Saint Richard of Chichester who died in 1253.

The revisers at the time of the Restoration had a new situation to deal with. There was a popular call for the recognition as a martyr of the dead king, Charles I, beheaded in 1649. There was political expedience too in encouraging the cult of the martyr. And, quite apart from what popular or political demands dictated, the Restoration church leaders were men who venerated a king whom they believed to have died for the Church of which they were adherents. A recent Anglican report maintains that

> King Charles is a clear example of popular canonisation; in which Church, State and popular feeling concurred, and that with a vehemence surprising to the modern generation.[28]

Assuming for one moment that the report is right and the honour paid to Charles amounted to canonisation (but see below for another view), what procedure could the Church adopt to achieve this canonisation where there were no precedents, all previous canonisation for some four hundred years or so having been by express papal authority?

A precedent could be found in Ireland in the 'canonisation' of Saint Richard of Dundalk by George Dowdall who became Archbishop of Armagh in 1544. The same Anglican report tells the story thus:

> The King (Henry VIII) was not then in communion with the Pope, who tried in vain to appoint a rival. By one of his first acts, Dowdall summoned a provincial, not a diocesan, Synod to Drogheda, 20 June, 1545. There, after a procession to the High Cross and back, he canonised a predecessor (1347–60) in the see, Richard FitzRalph, as St Richard of Dundalk; his festival was ordered to be observed on 27 June. It is true that the cult of this good bishop, celebrated not only as a theologian and preacher but for shining personal holiness, had been maintained in Dundalk and neighbourhood for more than a century and a half, ever since the archbishop's bones had been brought back from Avignon, where he died in 1360. It is true that, as Roman Catholic historians point out, the feast of St. Richard Rowey, Archbishop of Armagh, unconfirmed by the Papacy, occurs

on 14 March in the Antiphonary of Armagh, and that this is older than Dowdall's Synod of 1545. But in confirming a local cult familiar to all, and in providing for a public celebration of the feast with nine lessons on a definite but new date, Archbishop Dowdall would seem to have explicitly maintained, in separation from the Papacy, the older functions of the episcopate in decreeing the public recognition and veneration of a saint.[29]

Whether the seventeenth-century English churchmen who included King Charles in their Prayer Book knew about Archbishop Dowdall's action a hundred years or so before we do not know. At first sight however their own action may seem very similar. As with Richard FitzRalph, so with Charles, there was popular demand, a degree of veneration already in existence. As with FitzRalph, propers (collect, epistle, and gospel) were provided. As with the Irish saint, the celebration of the feast was ordered by a wider ecclesiastical authority than the archbishop acting alone (in Ireland a provincial synod; in England convocation and parliament). But in the case of Charles there was no solemn liturgical occasion, always a mark of canonisation both in the Roman practice and in that Irish case when canonisation only followed 'after a procession to the High Cross and back'. Charles' name was entered in the calendar of the Book of Common Prayer and a special order of service for his feast (30 January) was also enjoined.[30] Was canonisation specifically in mind? Not necessarily. For the service in honour of Charles belongs to a set of services for rather special occasions of national interest—Restoration Day, Gunpowder Plot Day, to name but two—and all these events were likewise inserted into the calendar. It clearly cannot have been their intention to canonise Charles II whose Restoration was being commemorated, for he was still alive! The naming of Charles I in the calendar need have indicated no more than a reminder to use the special service. It may be wondered, if canonisation was intended, why Charles is never called Saint Charles, for the Prayer Book is not hesitant so to name the great heroes of the faith. The naming of Charles in the calendar can be understood in one of three ways. It may have been a conscious, if somewhat irregular, act of canonisation. Or it may have been a conscious decision to commemorate the martyr-king while rejecting formal canonisation in a reformed church. Or it may have been an action into which no real thought of canonisation, in favour or against it, entered. We do not know which and consequently must be more cautious than the Anglican report which declares with great confidence that the service and the naming in the calendar was

> as genuine canonisation—that, too, of a martyr—as the historic church can show, Convocation, Parliament, and popular acclaim acting in passionate unity.

It is interesting, though it is difficult to know whether a conclusion can reasonably be drawn, to note that Charles is singled out for unique treatment. Were canonisation in mind, Archbishop William Laud would have been as strong a candidate. Like Charles he had died a martyr's death. Perhaps he would have been controversial in a way that Charles, in the euphoria of the Restoration, was not. In any case, his would have been an inappropriate inclusion in a collection of services for royal occasions.

The observance of King Charles the Martyr's Day has been a controversial one, at some times in the Church's history commending itself to the majority, but more recently not. For some it has had a great emotional appeal, as to the Tractarians, and Keble wrote, as only Keble could:

> Praise to our God! not cottage hearths alone,
> And shades impervious to the proud world's glare,
> Such witness yield: a monarch from his throne
> Springs to his Cross, and finds his glory there.[31]

But there does not seem to have been any desire by the men of the Oxford Movement to revive a regular process of canonisation in the Anglican Church. It would not have been entirely surprising had they wanted to see other seventeenth-century figures so recognised, especially as their attachment to the way the early Church organised itself would have demonstrated to them that papal authority was not needed for canonisation. However they were content to be loyal to the Prayer Book and its provisions, though the generation of Anglo-catholics who followed them were not so happy.[32] By the turn of the century, the increased liturgical commemoration of saints, with churches and chapels where there was a daily Eucharist, together with a more catholic attitude to doctrine widespread, it was to be expected that there would be pressure for a new attitude to canonisation. But among 'High churchmen' there was also a desire not to add to the matters that already divided the Anglican and Roman churches. A decision to canonise, against papal authority, would have been a move in the wrong direction, though Anglicans of this type, in using Roman service books increasingly from the early decades of the present century, happily commemorated Roman saints of the post-Reformation era.

The twentieth century has witnessed a change in emphasis, resulting partly from increasing doubt about old formulations of doctrine concerning the dead and their present state and, consequently, about the whole question of formal canonisation. But such a change has been very recent, at least in England,[33] and the action of Archbishop Cosmo Gordon Lang in 1935 on the fiftieth anniversary of the consecration of Edward King, a much loved Bishop of Lincoln, spiritual director and defender of catholic theology and practice in the Church of England, was well in advance of its time, to the extent that most of those present probably had no idea of what, in terms of historical precedent, was happening. The Anglican report already quoted describes the event:

> The Archbishop of Canterbury (Lang) celebrated a solemn Eucharist in Lincoln Cathedral, at which, before a large and important congregation, the collect, epistle and gospel were proper to Edward King. This is a direct 'raising to the altar', an overt case of 'canonisation' technically as may be; whether the archbishop understood his own act is uncertain but probable; the Bishop of Lincoln (Nugent Hicks) realised it clearly, prepared it deliberately, and forthwith issued the propers for use in the diocese on March 8 at the will of incumbents.

Names of many men and women not canonised by the Roman church are now being advanced in the Church of England. If the action at Lincoln described above or that at Drogheda four centuries ago do constitute canonisation, then the Church of England is now close to undertaking something that at national level it has not done since the days of the Dark Ages when canonisations were last made without the pope's approval. But what such 'canonisation' would mean is a question still to be considered. And before that must come the significant shift of 1928 of which the next chapter will speak.

Within the Roman Catholic Church there has been no significant shift in the way that saints are canonised in the years since the Reformation. The papacy has canonised the Roman Catholic martyrs of the Reformation era, English men and women among them, most notably Thomas More, Chancellor of England, and John Fisher, Cardinal Bishop of Rochester, both executed on the instructions of Henry VIII in 1535 and now commemorated annually on 22 June. Recent reforms, while 'down-grading' the significance in proving sanctity of miracles at the intercession of the departed hero, have not entirely eliminated them from the consideration of each case. They are still seen as a heavenly confirmation of the earthly indication that here was a life lived in God's power and favour. Nor have the reforms of the Second Vatican Council led to a restoration to the bishops or the bishops-in-synod of any rights in this matter. Canonisation by the pope alone remains the sole means of the recognition of heroic sanctity in the Roman Communion.

# 6 *A Significant Shift*

i

If any date could be said to mark a change in Anglican practice, it would be 1928, even though that date represents the apparent failure of proposals published several years before. What has come to be referred to as the '1928 Prayer Book' was known at first as the 'Deposited Book' and was presented to parliament twice, in 1927 and 1928, and on both occasions rejected. The reasons for the failure of the book to become a new *Book of Common Prayer* are many and complicated,[1] but certainly among them was the objection of the 'Evangelical' or 'Low-church' party to the changes in those parts of the liturgy that related to the saints and the departed. Though the changes in this area did not go as far as the 'Anglo-catholic' or 'High-church' party desired, the Evangelicals were certainly right to detect in what was proposed a quite significant shift. The changes were quite reasonably said to be as much doctrinal as liturgical.

2 November was designated in the calendar 'The Commemoration of All Souls'. This was, of course, an ancient observance of the Church dating back to the end of the tenth century, but it had disappeared from the calendar of the English church at the Reformation, though All Saints' Day (1 November) had been retained. The implication for doctrine was clear. Whereas in the *Book of Common Prayer* all God's faithful servants departed were recalled when the collect for All Saints' Day reminded God that he had knit together his 'elect in one communion and fellowship', in the book of 1928 the departed were divided into the 'saints' in a presumably more technical, though never defined, sense and the 'rest' in whatever state they might be. The great divide, unknown in the early Church, knocked down at the Reformation, was restored and Anglicanism came a good deal closer to the Roman Church's position. All Souls' Day was provided with collect, epistle, and gospel, the collect asking God to

> grant to the faithful departed all the unsearchable benefits of thy Son's passion; that in the day of his appearing they may be manifested as thy true children.

This was direct and specific prayer for the dead and the words employed were not much different from those in use in the Roman Church at the time. Far more Anglican in flavour were two prayers in the 'Occasional Prayers' which, under the heading 'A Commemoration of the Faithful Departed' and with a bidding 'Let us remember before God the faithful departed' (note that never did it say that the departed were to be *prayed for*), asked God

> to shed forth upon thy whole Church in Paradise and on earth the bright beams of thy light and heavenly comfort

and to

> multiply . . . , to those who rest in Jesus, the manifold blessings of thy love, that the good work which thou didst begin in them may be perfected unto the day of Jesus Christ.[2]

It is not entirely clear what is meant by the 'Church in Paradise'. Is Paradise heaven? Or is it purgatory? Or is it a name that covers them both? Or does it simply represent an agnosticism about the state of the departed before the final judgement that prefers not to be committed to anything too specific? Or is it simply a convenient name because it permits different interpretations, nearly always necessary in Anglican liturgy? Were it not that by introducing All Souls' Day the revisers had moved in the opposite direction, it would have perhaps seemed that they were reinforcing the view of the early Church and the Reformers that the dead cannot be categorised into the saintly and the 'not-quite-so-saintly'. They do, however, like the prayers in the Roman liturgy, pray only for the faithful among the dead. Prayer for those whose faith is a matter of speculation is not permitted.

The Alternative Order of Holy Communion in the book of 1928 was one of its most controversial features and the rite in its entirety has seldom been used. But the Intercession (since incorporated in *Alternative Services, Series 1 and Series 1 & 2 Revised* and therefore legally permitted) was used a good deal from the start. The shift in emphasis here is best illustrated by setting the words used to recall the dead in the two rites, 1662 (*Book of Common Prayer*) and 1928, alongside each other.

| *1662* | *1928* |
| --- | --- |
| And we also bless thy holy name for all thy servants departed this life in thy faith and fear; beseeching thee to give us grace so to follow their good examples, that with them we may be partakers of thy heavenly kingdom: | And we commend to thy gracious keeping, O Lord, all thy servants departed this life in thy faith and fear; beseeching thee to grant them everlasting light and peace. And here we give thee most high praise and hearty thanks for all thy Saints, who have been the chosen vessels of thy grace, and lights of the world in their several generations; and we pray, that rejoicing in their fellowship, and following their good examples, we may be partakers with them of thy heavenly kingdom. |

Again, the 1928 version separates saints and the rest of the faithful departed. It also commends the departed to God and asks for them light and peace, whereas the *Book of Common Prayer* simply blesses God for them. In both versions the examples (in 1662 of all God's servants departed, in 1928 of the saints) are called to mind. That 1928 version owes a good deal to Cranmer's first rite of 1549. That had of course been abandoned in 1552 when even the version in the *Book of Common Prayer* did not find a place.[3]

The emphasis in the Burial Service remained unchanged, but, among the new material, one prayer was specifically for the dead.

> We pray to thee for those whom we love, but see no longer. Grant them thy peace; let light perpetual shine upon them; and in thy loving wisdom and almighty power work in them the good purpose of thy perfect will.

Two traditional formulae for commending the departed also found their way into the proposed book:

> Rest eternal grant unto them, O Lord: and let light perpetual shine upon them.[4]
>
> May the souls of the faithful, through the mercy of God, rest in peace.[5]

But a change, as significant as any, was in the rubrics. One of those at the end of the Burial Service begins

> When there is a special celebration of the Holy Communion on the day of the Burial

and another, after the collect, epistle, and gospel for All Souls' Day notes

> that this service may be used on any day when desired, not being a Holy-day, or a day within the octave of Christmas, Easter or Whitsunday.

To a suspicious Evangelical, these rubrics seemed to look rather too much like the return of *Requiem* masses, masses for the dead. Of course there was nothing in the texts to imply that the Eucharist was offered 'for the dead', but the direction in which things had moved was clear. On the majority of days in the year the priest might choose to make the dead the 'intention' (if he used such a term) of the Eucharist and read a collect, setting the theme for the service, which asked that the faithful departed be granted the benefits of Christ's passion. No wonder there was opposition.

The saints, in the sense of the great heroes of the faith, received new treatment. The mention they received in the Intercession at the Eucharist has already been set out. In addition a new 'proper preface' on major saints' days inserted into the Eucharistic Prayer itself declared that

> in the righteousness of thy saints [thou] hast given us an ensample of godly living, and in their blessedness a glorious pledge of the hope of our calling.

One of the Occasional Prayers, drawing on Cranmer's book of 1549, is worth quoting in full because it sums up well the place in the life of the Church that the revisers clearly thought the saints should have.

> O God of the spirits of all flesh, we praise and magnify thy holy name for all thy servants who have finished their course in thy faith and fear, for the Blessed Virgin Mary, for the holy Patriarchs, Prophets, Apostles, and Martyrs, and for all other thy righteous servants known to us or unknown; and we beseech thee that, encouraged by their examples, and strengthened by their fellowship, we also may be found meet to be partakers of the inheritance of the saints in light; through the merits of thy Son Jesus Christ our Lord.[6]

In speaking of encouragement from the example of the saints, the prayer simply reiterates the emphasis of the Reformers that saints are to be recalled because of their godly lives from which we may try to learn and which we may seek to imitate. But in placing alongside that the strength that comes from their fellowship (as the 1928 Intercession at the Eucharist does as well), the revisers were giving a very new sort of emphasis to Anglican liturgy. They do not speak of the prayers of the saints. Indeed 'fellowship' is nowhere defined. Presumably, however, if it is true Christian fellowship, prayer will form a part of it, unless fellowship in heaven is unrecognisable from fellowship on earth. Hesitantly, and almost in disguise, therefore, the revisers were giving liturgical expression to that conviction expressed by theologians of both the seventeenth and nineteenth centuries that the departed do indeed pray for the living, even if it is somehow improper for the living to prompt them to do so. The prayer above is also typical of what the revisers seem to have been trying to do in the way that it singles out Mary, the mother of Jesus, and the great categories of heroes for special mention. The Church was being called to talk less of 'all [God's] servants departed this life', but to make more of its great ones.

As a natural consequence of this, the revisers made greater provision for the observance of saints' days by including collects, epistles, and gospels for 'black-letter' days. Suddenly, not only the biblical figures who long had been 'red-letter' saints, but a host of heroic and saintly figures down the ages could be recalled and celebrated as they could not have been (legally) before. The calendar suddenly became significant. It mattered not a bit that it was full of such unlikely people as Saint Brice, Saint Evurtius, and Saint Malo when there was in any case no provision for celebrating these feasts. But now that collects and readings made liturgical observance possible a happier selection needed to be made. The revisers met this need, to some extent at least, in a new calendar.[7] The individual additions and alterations in the new book may each seem relatively insignificant. But, put together, they represent a considerable shift, both in bringing the communion of saints in its widest sense into the centre of Anglican worship, where before it had been on the fringe, and also in laying stress on 'fellowship', with all that implies, as much as on example.

In making such provision, the revisers were of course simply responding to pressure. Belief in some sort of prayer for the dead had already taken hold of a wide section of the Church, by no means only the identifiably Anglo-catholic element. This attitude had accelerated a good deal through and beyond the years of the First World War when it had arisen as a response to great emotional need. But in Anglo-catholic circles, illegal books of various kinds, normally rather poor translations either of the Roman Missal or of pre-Reformation English service-books, were well established, and in these the prayers of the saints were sought and the dead prayed for in such words as these:

> Grant . . . that the intercession of holy Mary Mother of God, and of all the holy Apostles, Martyrs, Confessors and Virgins, and of all thine elect, may everywhere cause us to rejoice; that while we call to mind their merits, we may perceive their advocacy.
>
> O Lord Jesus Christ, King of glory, deliver the souls of all the faithful departed from the pains of hell and from the depths of the pit.[8]

Churches which used these books did not, on the whole, ever adopt the book of 1928, even though, after its failure to receive parliamentary approval and therefore to become the *Book of Common Prayer*, the bishops, on their own limited authority, allowed the use of parts of it. The churches where it was used most tended to be those of the broad undoctrinaire 'central-churchmanship', 'typical Church of England', neither 'high' nor 'low', that found the Prayer Book unsatisfactory but would not deviate from authority. The use of the book of 1928 in such churches right through until the appearance of new liturgical forms in the 1960's and 1970's, which have not in any case yet entirely superseded it, has inevitably meant the propagation of the sort of views it implied on the departed and the saints to a far wider cross-section of Anglicanism in England.

## ii

The calendar of 1928 set about trying to provide the Church of England with a more representative group of saints to honour. Many of those listed in the *Book of Common Prayer* not surprisingly disappeared without trace. Nothing in any case had really been known about Agatha, Blaise (Blasius), Nicomede, Prisca, or Valentine. Martin, the fourth-century Bishop of Tours, was a significant figure, but not so significant that he required two feasts, so that of his 'translation' was removed. Very little had been known of Lucian of Antioch, except that he died a martyr's death under the Diocletian persecution, presuming that we must discount the amusing tale that he had been drowned in the sea and that his body had been brought to land by a dolphin; nor of Evurtius (or Enurchus) except that he was an early (fourth-century?) Bishop of Orleans; nor of Malo (or Machutus) save that he worked in the area now called Saint-Servan; nor of Lucy of Syracuse except that she, like Lucian, suffered in the Diocletian persecution, and she is also named in the canon of the Roman Mass.[9] Rather more is known about Saint Lambert of Maastricht: he was a zealous missionary bishop for thirty years in Belgium in the eighth century and was martyred; and about Saint Silvester, a fourth-century pope, one of the first non-martyrs to be venerated as a saint in Rome. Both these were worthy Christian saints, but not of much interest or consequence to the English church.

Saint Brice (or Britius), however, provided a rather different problem. He was one of Martin of Tours' clergy and succeeded him as bishop in 397. Donald Attwater writes of him that

> after allowing for exaggeration and malice, Brice still seems to have been of insubordinate and troublesome character; and, whatever the true circumstances, he had to leave his see *c.* 430, and was in exile for seven years.[10]

He did later return and mend his ways, but it does seem likely that he was venerated more for his association with Saint Martin than for his own sanctity. So there was good reason for omitting him; and even better for striking out both feasts of Saint Edward, the ninth-century King of the West Saxons. The legend goes that he was on his way to visit his half-brother Ethelred when he was set upon by Ethelred's retainers and stabbed before he could dismount from his horse. His was not really a martyrdom. It was simply an unjust death, which is not the same thing at all.

There would seem to have been three principles at work behind these omissions. The first is simply one of lack of historical basis for a cult. They simply did not know enough about some of the entries for any sort of intelligent commemoration of them to be made. The second is one of relevance. However much may have been known about the sanctity or heroism of men like Lambert and Silvester, somehow its impact was bound to remain small on men and women of the twentieth century living in a land with which they had had no connections. The third is the more fundamental one of sanctity. How did Brice or Edward of the West Saxons qualify for the title 'saint'? Where there was doubt, the name was thought best omitted.

Bearing in mind these principles and turning to the saints of the Prayer Book calendar who are retained in the book of 1928, there are surprises in store. Whatever was it that allowed Margaret of Antioch (20 July) and Katherine of Alexandria (25 November) to remain? Donald Attwater writes of Margaret:

> There is no positive evidence that she ever existed. Her story is simply a fictitious romance. It relates that in the reign of Diocletian a pagan priest at Antioch in Pisidia had a Christian daughter, Margaret. She rejected the advances of the prefect Olybrius, who thereupon denounced her as a Christian. The ordeals she then suffered are of the most fabulous description (including being swallowed by Satan in the form of a dragon); finally she was beheaded. This farrago professes to have been written by an eye-witness, Margaret's attendant, Theotimus. There are points of resemblance between the cultus of this Margaret and of Katherine of Alexandria.[11]

It comes as no great surprise therefore to discover that there is no evidence at all for the existence of Saint Katherine either

> outside the mind of some Greek writer who first composed what he intended to be simply an edifying romance.[12]

But both Margaret and Katherine retain their place in the calendar of 1928, as do Fabian (20 January), Faith (6 October), Giles (1 September), Leonard (6 November), and Swithun (15 July), whom, though they existed, we know practically nothing about, and Remi (or Remigius) (1 October) and Vincent (22 January) who, though their lives are well-attested, are not of great relevance in England. Crispin (25 October), a quite legendary figure of whom nothing is known, received special treatment in that his equally legendary brother, Crispinian, about whom nothing is known either, joined him in the calendar. At first sight the revisers seem to have done a very inadequate task. But gradually more principles emerge.

One of these was to retain the name of any saint to whom there are a large number of churches dedicated in this country. Great saints in medieval devotion are among the least reliable historically, but great saints in medieval devotion gave their names to a large number of churches. A second further principle was to include at least one great saint of each great country, though inevitably this meant in practice of every great European country, for there were no canonised saints to represent the vast new areas of the world. This principle led not only to a reprieve for the likes of Vincent (representing Spain) and Remi (representing France), but also to the inclusion to represent

Scandinavia of Anskar, a ninth-century missionary in Sweden and Denmark (3 February). The 1957 Anglican report already quoted[13] asks of the inclusion of Anskar:

> It is a neighbourly and catholic intent, but is it sound? Anskar will never mean much to anybody except the small and specialised group who work for closer relations with the Church of Sweden.

It is to the additions to the calendar that we must now turn. Two more principles immediately emerge. The first is the inclusion of a number of saints of universal interest for one reason or another omitted from the *Book of Common Prayer.* The earliest Christian centuries are represented by Ignatius of Antioch, that very early martyr who had probably known the apostles (17 December), Polycarp of Smyrna, the story of whose moving martyrdom has already been told[14] (26 January), and Irenaeus of Lyons, perhaps the most important theologian of the second century and a disciple of Polycarp (28 June). But the omission of Justin Martyr is strange. For he was the most significant Christian apologist of the second century and the first of whose written works notable parts are extant.

The great flourishing of patristic theology is represented by Athanasius of Alexandria, the great opponent of Arianism (2 May), Basil of Caesarea, one of the four great Greek 'doctors of the church' (14 June), John Chrysostom of Constantinople, another of those four and famed above all else as a preacher (27 January), and Leo of Rome, a strong pope and defender of early orthodoxy (11 April). Among those who could claim great scholarship and theological significance in that age, only Gregory of Nazianzus fails to be included.

The importance of monasticism within the Church is reflected in the inclusion of Antony of Egypt, the third-century hermit regarded as the founder of monasticism (17 January), Bernard of Clairvaux, a founder of the twelfth-century Cistercian order that had such wide influence in England at such great abbeys as Fountains and Rievaulx (20 August), and that most famous and popular of medieval saints, Francis of Assisi (4 October). A glaring omission among the monastic additions was that of Dominic, who a few years before Francis formed his community began the work of the Friars Preachers, the Dominicans.

Catherine of Siena, who died in 1380, is included as a sole representative of a great mystical tradition in the Church. Catherine was not of course its greatest exponent, but, unlike, say, Teresa of Avila, she was a pre-Reformation figure and that, for the revisers, was important. Monica, the mother of Saint Augustine of Hippo (4 May), presumably stands for Christian motherhood in a calendar populated by saints pledged to virginity, even though she can be in no way typical of motherhood and many would think her a somewhat unedifying symbol, despite her devotion. Clement of Alexandria (4 December) is the most interesting entry. Clement, who belongs to the end of the third century, was recognised in the early centuries as a saint (in the days, of course, before formal canonisation), but his works were later judged unorthodox and the Church ceased (and the Roman Church still ceases) to regard him as a saint. This did not deter the 1928 revisers. He is, so to speak, a decanonised, rather than an uncanonised, entry in the calendar.

The second principle of inclusion is nationality. The proportion of British saints is increased and some glaring omissions rectified. For Ireland, Patrick, its great fifth-century missionary bishop and patron saint (17 March) is brought in. For Scotland, two very early missionary saints, Columba, sixth-century abbot of Iona (9 June), and Ninian, fifth-century bishop in Galloway (16 September), are included, but the omission of Margaret, Queen of Scotland, is surprising, for she is much more obviously a Scottish national saint than any other.

Nine new English saints appear, five of them of the seventh century. Aidan (31 August) and Cuthbert (20 March), both Bishops of Lindisfarne, Hilda, abbess of Whitby (17 November), and Oswald, King of Northumbria (5 August) all deserve their place, though among their north-country contemporaries any of Benedict Biscop, missionary abbot of Wearmouth, Paulinus, sent by Augustine from the south, and Wilfrid of Ripon, pro-Roman Bishop of York and Hexham, could as justifiably have been included. Still in the seventh century, Theodore of Tarsus, a reforming Archbishop of Canterbury (19 September), represents the south, but a better choice might have been Birinus, missionary Bishop of Dorchester (in Oxfordshire) who played a vital role in building up the church in the south Midlands.

Aldhelm, missionary Bishop of Sherborne (25 May), is the sole representative of the eighth century. Attractive figure as he is, he was not by any means one of the great evangelisers and he may have won his place in the calendar simply because of the unsuitability of most eighth-century candidates. But the following century sees the inclusion of a far greater west-country figure, Alfred the Great (26 October). Of that inclusion, the Anglican report of 1957, commented:

> It is strange how so great a king, man, Christian, and missionary to his people should have escaped kalendrical and liturgical recognition for so many centuries. If the 1928 book were formally authoritative, it could be said that this was a clear case of 'canonisation' by the two provinces of the Church of England.

This is not quite accurate. Certainly Alfred never came to be recognised as canonised by authority, whether of pope or provincial synod, and, as the report claims, this is indeed strange. But 'kalendrical recognition' there certainly was, though how widespread may be doubted, as the entry already referred to in the eleventh-century Wessex calendar, *Sancti Eadfridi confessoris*, indicates.[15]

The only other pre-conquest saint to be included is St. Wulfstan of Worcester (19 January). If Dom David Knowles' judgement is correct, Wulfstan's inclusion is well justified despite his apparent obscurity. Knowles describes Wulfstan as

> a most attractive figure, too little known to his countrymen . . .; the last, and certainly one of the greatest, of the (early) bishops of pure English blood and culture.[16]

Of the great medieval English saints, only Anselm, Archbishop of Canterbury and theologian right at the beginning of the era (21 April), is given a place. The omission once again of a later Archbishop of Canterbury, Thomas Becket, was perhaps inevitable. The Reformation Church had made such a point of excluding him that to restore him to the calendar would have been too controversial. But perhaps Becket's contemporary, Aelred of Rievaulx, a most attractive English medieval monastic figure, might have found his way into the calendar. The new entries of English saints end with Anselm who died in 1109. There are few outstanding canonised figures of the Middle Ages in England to include. Perhaps Edmund Rich of Abingdon (died 1240), who combined an impressive episcopate and statesmanship with a devout and holy life, would have been a suitable candidate.

Not as suitable or obvious however as Robert Grosseteste (died 1253), but he, as already noted,[17] had never been canonised by the pope. His local cult had however been at least as official and widespread as that of Alfred, so the revisers might have 'stretched the point', even though it emerges, in general, that another of their principles was to include only recognised canonised figures. Because of this no Reformation or post-Reformation figure in the Anglican Church is included. Formal canonisation is the norm, but even that was not enough to allow a post-Reformation Roman Catholic saint to be included. While rejecting papal authority, the revisers remained loyal to the principle that saints for inclusion in the calendar must have papal approval and must also belong to the centuries when the English church was in communion with the see of Rome. The calendar of 1928 was therefore bereft both of the great Anglican divines—George Herbert, Richard Hooker, John Keble *et al*—and also of the great post-Reformation Roman saints—Francis of Sales, John of the Cross, Teresa of Avila among them. The first group, however, achieved a degree of commemoration on 8 November, the octave day of All Saints', which was designated 'Saints, Martyrs, Missionaries, and Doctors of the Church of England'.

The revisers did nothing to alter the convention that only biblical figures of the New Testament were to be treated as 'red-letter' saints. They added to their number Saint Mary Magdalen, the first witness of the resurrection (22 July), but failed to include, even as a 'black-letter' saint, Joseph, the husband of Mary, despite the recommendation of the Anglo-catholics. Though no doubt they had a reason, it is not an obvious one. Anglicans abroad certainly failed to see it.

# 7 *All One Body*

## i

Throughout the history of the Church there has been some attempt to retain a theological rationale for whatever commemoration of the departed a particular age has adopted. The Church in the twentieth century has to face the same theological task if liturgy and devotion are not to be divorced from theology. Some might consider the subject a peripheral one when such basic Christian beliefs as the existence and nature of God are in question,[1] but to dismiss the doctrine of the communion of saints as speculative theology would be to miss the point. Far from being simply a matter of traditional rivalries, it is one of the issues of Christian belief that the believer or half-believer is least able to ignore or dismiss as the speculation of theologians. Death will come to every man and woman, and nearly every man and woman has been profoundly affected by the death of one to whom they have been close. The questioning that must arise from such experience and such fears must be for many just the urgent and important issues that demand some sort of answer. Of course it is right that this is an age that formulates questions as fundamental as to challenge the existence and nature of God. But, when all is said and done, questions about death and life beyond are questions about God and, more specifically, about the individual and his final confrontation with God. The search for the truth is therefore worth pursuing, but it is a difficult task to work within the theological confusion of the late twentieth century.

Christian belief in this, as in all matters, looks back to the Bible for its foundations. But the picture that emerges is a very confusing one and, even if it were possible to find behind the confusion some clear and definite pattern of belief, drawn presumably from some sort of synthesis of the divergent views of many centuries and cultural influences, that pattern would have only a limited usefulness for twentieth-century man. But in fact such a synthesis is not attainable. First of all it is clear that the evidence, or lack of it, in the Old Testament does not conform to what Christian orthodoxy, emerging (or so it thought) out of the New Testament, has believed. The hope beyond death of most of the psalmists, constantly re-emphasising that the one place where Yahweh can be of no help to men is in Sheol, the place of the dead,[2] is very different from the faith of the Book of Maccabees, which is not far removed from the pictures that Jesus and Paul accepted. There is a sufficiently dramatic shift in Jewish eschatology between the typical Old Testament view of Sheol and the general tone of the New Testament that synthesis is out of the question. Searches in the Old Testament or the Apocrypha for texts on prayer for the departed are therefore quite as irrelevant as they are unfruitful.[3] But, turning to the New Testament, we are confronted with as great a problem. The new way of looking at the subject, that has replaced the rather gloomy belief in Sheol, is just as far removed from any twentieth-century view of things, because of the centrality to its argument of an expected imminent end of the world, a *parousia* just round the corner. Our problem is not just that the *parousia* has not happened, but that we do not expect it to happen, either just round the corner or in the far future, in the way that the biblical writers believed.

There is also a good deal of divergence within the New Testament itself, not surprisingly so, though we have become so used to the synthesising process in biblical theology that it does not strike us as it should. Sometimes it is difficult to describe the divergences as less than contradictions, especially in relation to the question of judgement. Certainly there is development and restatement in the light of the fact that the Lord did not come soon bringing the kingdom of God in the way the first Christians expected. Paul's different letters, spread over many years, reveal a patient restatement in response to this challenge. John's gospel reveals a Christian theology that has already begun to express the idea of eternity in very different terms.[4] Unless we believe that there is a particular date when revelation stopped, the evidence for development and restatement in the New Testament will encourage us to believe that this is still a legitimate, indeed a necessary task. But, in doing so, we have to keep before us the important fact that the diverse biblical images are not in any case to be regarded as any more than symbols, for even when they were written they had that status. All eschatological talk must be symbolic, and recognisably so to those who employ it. As Emil Brunner says:

> It is obvious that the prophets and Jesus Himself do not hesitate to use these symbols in the plainest and most daring manner, because obviously their whole concern is to assert God's personal character, His speaking to us, in contrast with every kind of abstraction.[5]

It is in that sort of light that such compelling visual images as the parable of the sheep and the goats,[6] or talk of the last trumpet when all shall be changed in a flash,[7] must be seen. Whatever we want to say today will, of course, likewise be clothed in symbolism—there is no escaping it.

Although development and restatement began in New Testament times and continued right through the history of the Church, the task has accelerated, and become a far more fundamental reconstruction, since the scientific revolution of the eighteenth century. The criticisms that have exposed the limits to the usefulness of the biblical material in our quest apply as much to most of the arguments of later generations before the cultural upheavals of the last two centuries. Most theologians will therefore find it difficult to go along with Karl Rahner that our starting point

> is always the doctrine proposed by the ordinary and the extraordinary *magisterium* of the Church to the faithful and to the theologian alike, the content of revelation in Scripture and Tradition. The doctrine proposed by the *magisterium*, once the theologian has determined what it is, . . . becomes the unquestionable foundation for all further efforts by the theologian.[8]

And so the attempt must proceed over fresh ground, nevertheless taking seriously the conviction of the New Testament and the succeeding Christian centuries that all that man wants to say about his death, and life beyond it, is somehow transformed and put in a new perspective by the life and death of Jesus of Nazareth, and by the conviction of those who knew him that God raised him from the dead.

Any restatement is likely to be more tentative and provisional than in the past. With Dennis Nineham, the twentieth-century thinker will find himself conceding

> Ours is an age acutely and healthily aware of the limits of its capacity to speak intelligibly about the extra-natural, and we shall perhaps distrust our ability to say more than a very little, by biblical

standards, about such topics as the end of history and its supernatural aftermath. Our experience of God may compel us to repeat after Mother Julian and T. S. Eliot our conviction that 'all shall be well and all manner of thing shall be well', but we may well feel incompetent to specify further and produce any equivalent for the vivid and often detailed biblical portrayals of the coming and character of the kingdom.[9]

The need for a more tentative approach has implications for the language of the liturgy. The theologian has always had a problem in finding a theological rationale for the beliefs that have found expression in the prayers of the faithful,[10] but the problem is perhaps more acute than ever before. For a whole century eschatological talk has been subjected to radical restatement. Yet in liturgy and devotion there has been no indication at all that some ideas are obsolete and some untenable. In parts of the Church where prayer to the saints is encouraged, such prayers are offered without any thought about whether this makes sense at all. In parts of the Church where prayer for the dead is common, the prayers continue to seek for the dead 'rest and peace' without any thought as to whether these are the most appropriate attributes to seek for them. In parts of the Church where prayer for the dead has been strongly discouraged, this disapproval has become part of the unchallengeable assumptions for which the particular party stands. The fossilising of views of life after death and the saints, by making them part of the 'party packages', is a further obstacle to more creative thinking. When some attempt is made to relate prayer to modern theological insights, as in the Doctrine Commission Report of 1971,[11] the words they suggest and employ receive little attention and are dismissed as shabby compromises, churchmen imagining that the formulae suggested are a subtle amalgam of irreconcilable old views rather than an attempt, irrespective of past quarrels, disputes, and party positions, to find words that give expression to what we can reasonably believe today.

## ii

Theological questions do not provide the only difficulties to a continued veneration of the saints. In the Protestant tradition and in the main stream of Anglican belief, saints have been honoured not for their lives in heaven now, but for their lives in this world in the past. In other words, it is their example that carries weight, not their prayers. Veneration of dead heroes is not of course an exclusively religious activity. Marxist Russia venerates Lenin in much the same way, while obviously having no thought of Lenin living today except in the continuance of the state that he helped to found. The only specifically Christian dimension to a view of saints that rejoices simply in the examples of saints is that, unlike for instance the Marxist, the Christian claims as the ultimate mark of worthiness not heroic deeds and exploits, intellectual excellence or even supreme revolutionary fervour, but sanctity.

If the saints are regarded chiefly as examples, the problem is the same one that has thrown into some confusion the Church's view of the significance of Jesus himself. Only in the last hundred years or so have people become fully aware of the implications of cultural conditioning for religious belief. But in this period our world view has undergone so dramatic a change that we find ourselves on the wrong side, or at least the other side, of a great divide that separates us from the pre-scientific world view that remained relatively static through the first sixteen hundred years of Christianity. Certainly a sixteenth-century saint, such as Teresa of Avila or Ignatius of Loyola, had a good deal more in common with Jesus and his contemporaries, from whom they were separated by fifteen hundred years, than with us from whom they are separated by a mere four hundred years. Our problem with Jesus is not that we know so little about him for sure. It is in part that there is so much about which we would dearly love guidance from him, but which the gospels cannot provide, because the matters that concern us were quite outside his experience. Jesus can tell us nothing very specific about what ethical response is appropriate in questions of abortion, capitalism, or other issues in which we recognise the possibility of a Christian perspective. There is a parallel between that and a good many of the saints. Their appeal and their usefulness to us as examples are limited by the fact that they were up against problems that are not burning issues for us, but failed to experience the issues which do matter desperately to us. That is a problem, for we do expect of our heroes that we can relate to them.

Nevertheless that is not the heart of the matter. The fundamental problem is not just that Jesus was never called upon to give a view on this or that particular issue, but his whole way of looking at things and experiencing what life had to offer was sufficiently different from ours that, first of all, we can hardly hope to 'get inside his skin', so to speak, to discover what it all really meant to him, and, secondly, that if we could by some miracle discover it, it would be of little help because his ideas and reactions and insights cannot simply be reconstructed to any useful purpose in our day.[12] What applies to Jesus applies equally well to the great figures of Christian history. They belong to their own times. They cannot, in Albert Schweitzer's striking phrase, 'contribute to the making of the present'. Cultural relativism does not only drive the Church to reassess the position of Jesus, but of his saints. When the Church talks of them as examples, it can be in only a very vague and general form. There can be no applying their methods and their standards in the search of twentieth-century man for the heroic sanctity that he may still admire in them, however much it may puzzle him and however little it may seem to speak to anything in his own experience.

There is one further problem of a similar kind. For a variety of reasons, in western society today we have far less regard for the past and its heroes than previous generations have done. No doubt this is partly a passing phenomenon, a cultural fashion whereby what one generation holds sacred another must decry. Yet there are reasons to believe that never again will the past be held in quite the reverence that has sometimes been the case. We are more aware than ever of the 'pastness' of the past, how its view of things was so alien to our own and the problems with which it contended so different from our own. But there are other reasons. The increasingly scientific approach to history, whereby the sort of cultural, and even nationalist, colourings with which it tended to be tinted are as far as possible eliminated, tends to expose the past for the mixture of good and bad that it was and prevent the idealising of past ages that has so often been the case. Similarly ideas of heroism now have to compete with a quite ruthless exploration into the lives, private as well as public, of famous figures, so that any flaw in their character will be fully exposed. It is all but impossible for any leader to seem 'larger than life'. Sometimes we may regret the extremes to which this modern sort of iconoclasm will go, and suspect that another generation will restore a greater degree of reverence to the heroes of the past, but it is quite certain that the pedestals on which great men and women are placed will never be so tall or so secure.

Such heroes as we have tend to be of a different sort. We do not look to the past for them, but to the present. The young idolise youthful figures in the world of popular music. The football crowds idolise their own contemporaries and do so only because of their particular skill, with no great respect for the total impact of their lives, for good or bad, on society. Particular politicians or revolutionary leaders catch the imagination of people—Mahatma Gandhi, Che Guavara, John and Robert Kennedy, for instance—but their cult is short lived. In fact it lasts only while they are actively engaged in political life or struggle and for a drastically short period of time after their death. In so far as we look for heroes at all, we seem to look for people who are engaged in living heroically the lives we want to live. Because these heroes are alive, they are up against the same problems, moved by the same events, shaped by the same experiences. We can identify with them. To some extent, we feel, if against all the pressures of twentieth-century living, these great men could live heroically, then we ought to be able to measure up in some way to them. But, when they die, they are no longer our contemporaries and therefore cannot be our inspiration. Indeed we regard their death not as the crowning glory of their career, but, quite the contrary, their death means failure. The causes for which they worked suffer severe set-backs by their death and this often seems to imply that they were pursuing the wrong policies. For instance, the death of Martin Luther-King did not secure support for his policy of peaceful resistance and of efforts for reconciliation between black and white in the United States. His death marked the turning point whereby many of his supporters moved over to support the more militant 'black power' leaders who had a very different philosophy. We have no real belief in the power of martyrdom in the twentieth-century western world. Even where a cult outlives its hero for a time, the hero's significance steadily declines rather than increases with the passing of years.

But the principal point is not the modernity or the temporary nature of our heroes, but that, on the whole, we do not seriously seek hero-figures at all. How can saints, figures of the past, often of the distant past, many of whom have been venerated chiefly because of the manner of their dying, make any impact in this sort of cultural atmosphere?

The inescapable 'pastness' of the saints will worry the Church less if it can rediscover a sense of the *communion* of saints, rather than simply an interest in individual holy people. Participation in the communion of saints involves recalling, and being encouraged by, Christian heroism and sanctity in every age in almost all conditions known to man, in the face of nearly every threat to life or to faith. It is the totality of what the saints have stood for that is important. Because the word 'example' is likely to be misunderstood if used in these terms, a better word is probably the biblical word 'witness'. The witness of God's holy ones down the ages is a striking testimony to us of God's concern, guidance, and power. The word 'witness' is additionally a useful and instructive one because, whereas to use the word 'example' is to concentrate on the saint and his achievements, to speak of witness is to empower the saint to point beyond himself to where his strength comes from, to the God of whose power at work in human life he is a witness.

What is the most appropriate word to describe the effect of this total witness of the saints through the ages? Imitation is not possible—cultural differences render it so and, in any case, one person cannot imitate the witness of two thousand years. The effect is more helpfully described in terms of 'encouragement'. We say not, 'Because the saints of the past behaved in such and such a way in this situation, I shall do the same', but, 'If the saints of the past in their situation found such and such to be the appropriate way to act, what is the appropriate way for me? God helped them to see the way forward and to remain faithful in doing it. He will do the same for me.'

It would be quite wrong to pretend that the significance of the past presses itself upon us as forcefully as it did in previous generations. Nevertheless Christianity remains tied to the past, and provided that it is secured in the right way this is both desirable and necessary. We do not know as much as we thought we knew about the historical Jesus. But we do know that within a community (or communities) of men and women, living under God and honouring the memory of Jesus Christ, there grew up in a very short time a society, the Church, in which a faith was proclaimed. The faith we now hold is recognisably the same faith, though not of course exactly the same. We know that our belief would not be what it is, had their faith not been what it was. That does not imply any sort of static faith. Even when the same words are used in different centuries and cultures, these words are filled with a variety of meaning. But it does imply that the saints are a link between us and that little band that preached a new relationship with God emerging from the saving events it discerned behind the life of Jesus. At very least that fact requires of us a profound thankfulness to God for his saints. We are thankful, therefore, because the saints are the links in the chain by which we are reminded of our spiritual origins in the 'Christ-event', but also—and this is just as important—because the lives of the saints adequately and richly witness to the fact that God's power and love, breaking through in the life of Jesus and its aftermath in a way that seems unparalleled, nevertheless is not limited to that age, but can break through again and again in different ways in different people within different cultures. And in that knowledge we experience encouragement.

## iii

It is against these questions and problems, as well as against its traditional theological controversies of many centuries, that the Christian Church seeks to evaluate its doctrine and practice in relation to those who have died. It is a difficult task to describe briefly what the Church today believes about life after death (for it involves just the sort of synthesis of views that we have tried to disentangle in relation to the Bible), but without this knowledge we cannot begin to examine what role the saints ought to have in the life and liturgy of the Church today.

Christian thinking has to face first the question of physical death. What is the spiritual significance of physical death? Death is highly significant, but not because of something dramatic that the Christian knows or even believes will happen then, but because his ignorance of what will happen then has a marked bearing upon his life in the present. The significance of death is in fact not so much for the hour of death, but for now. Fear perhaps, ignorance certainly, of the future beyond it, combined with an intuition that there are things which, if not done now in this life, can never be done, profoundly affect man's life in the world. Yet that is in some way a sub-Christian view. The man of *faith* does not attribute great finality to death, but looks beyond it, even if he remains silent, seeing nothing he can describe, because he is confident that God accompanies him there as he does so here. Meditating on what will happen to him at death, the man of faith is not alarmed. Death is not therefore significant for his way of living. He acts responsibly not because of fear of judgement, but because of love of God.

What then does talk of 'judgement' mean? We can attribute no more than a figurative character to the biblical picture, one of particular force and vividness, of a court of judgement and an actual visible separation of good and evil. Talk of judgement may at least be seen as implying revelation, disclosure, to man of his true self. Emil Brunner expresses it thus:

> Nothing further is needed but that the divine light should pierce man's being so that what is hidden—like the internal parts of the body under x-rays—becomes visible. This again is a metaphor implying the full disclosure of what has hither been concealed. 'It comes to light'—that is the essence of judgement. It is revealed—not for God: for how could anything have ever been concealed from Him?—but for ourselves. We shall stand naked and exposed, according to the truth of our being, with no concealing raiment . . . The sole decisive thing is the fact of manifestation.[13]

In this picture judgement is not a divine act. If there is judgement, it is judgement by man. He sees himself as he is and judges himself. Nevertheless God is not outside the picture, since it must be by an act of his grace that man can come to this self-knowledge in which true judgement is possible. As Brunner says, God's activity is 'manifestation'. Judgement is man's response. Judgement, as here described, is not necessarily an act of a single moment. If human personality reacts and develops beyond death in something like the way it does in this world, judgement of this sort will usually be a gradual process of becoming aware of the truth. An emphasis on immortality, and therefore on continuity, would probably indicate such a gradual process. But an emphasis on death as a moment of truth would of course envisage a more dramatic crisis point of change in which all is suddenly revealed. We cannot know which picture more precisely visualises what happens. Probably both have their place—dramatic moment and gradual change—for no event, however devastating, is ever entirely unrelated to what goes on before and after it.

But manifestation is not all that we imply by judgement. Judgement must also mean choice or decision. It is an inevitable outcome of manifestation that man is forced to think out his response to what has been revealed. He must make a choice. God does not sit back, so to speak, and simply await man's choice or decision. Because he loves, he is engaged in the decision-making process. He desires that man choose the way of life and he must press his case. To do otherwise would be to show indifference.

The decision is therefore made by man in dialogue with God. But still man makes a choice.

As such, judgement is part of this life, God and man in dialogue assisting man to greater maturity. But beyond death, at the crisis point or points, the revelation is more devastating and the judgement, the purging, the change and correction in course, correspondingly more radical. But, if judgement is seen in terms of growth and development, what is to be made of 'last judgement' at the end of time? The language of the *parousia* is symbolic, but is there still to be found in it for men and women of our world view any meaning behind the symbols? If it necessarily implies an end of the world by divine intervention, the Church today is very wary to go on using such language. For the end of the world would seem to be something it should leave to the scientists, uncertain as they are. If it necessarily means an end to the process of growth and development of the individual beyond death, the Church is also cautious, because it wants to maintain a belief in a dynamic God. Does not an end to growth spell death? It is a difficult question. On the one hand we want to stress growth, for growth means life. On the other hand we do not want to exclude the idea of achievable perfection. We do not want perfection always to be just outside our grasp, always still to be striven for. Perhaps we have to say that, although there will always be growth, as indeed there is always constant new life being generated in God, there comes a point where the direction of the growth is so firmly fixed that no fundamental choices remain to be made. The element of striving, the agitation that breeds on uncertainty, is therefore removed and a certain sort of peace and serenity takes over. Although there are always new things to discover and new growth to be experienced, the last choice has been made and perfection is already a reality. Now that need not be at death. Death may be a moment of dramatic decision, but it need not be the decision that excludes all other options and fundamental choices for the future. The biblical tension between the judgement of death and the final judgement pictures this difficult belief in a helpful way. As John Macquarrie puts it:

> Belief in a final judgement is the hope that what is now ambiguous will resolve itself and the advance of good over evil will decisively prevail.[14]

Such a view of judgement implies a constant growth. The use of the word 'growth' necessarily implies rejection of any totally final decision that freezes our relationship with God at the point of bodily death. As John Hick puts it:

> We must reject the traditional doctrine, both catholic and protestant, of the unalterability of the soul's state beyond death, the doctrine that there can be no 'second chance' of salvation beyond this life, no new and different moral decision, and no personal growth or development in response to further experiences.

He emphasises the need for more than simply this life, if a divine purpose of 'person-making' is to reach completion.

> If responsible life—the exercise of freedom through time in an environment which demands responses—is the basis of the person-making process, and if the divine intention in initiating this process is that it should be carried through to completion, it follows that responsible life must continue beyond bodily death.[15]

What is envisaged by 'growth' is therefore a sort of moral and spiritual development which proceeds continuously through infinite time, though not without end and goal. Man continues upon his eternal journey in search of the fullness of the richness of God. Along the journey there will be times of spectacular growth and times of apparent aridity. The tale that John Bunyan tells in *Pilgrim's Progress* captures the changing moods well. In other words, there will be in this eternal existence distinct phases in growth. Christian orthodoxy will not go as far as John Hick, who suggests a succession of lives lived within their different worlds, a modification of a reincarnation doctrine,[16] but it does emphasise the variety that gives growth within the eternal life of the journey, rather than the static monotony of some traditional views.

If after life is described in terms of continued growth towards maturity, or selfhood, which, when achieved or at least grasped, brings the Christian into a new and complete relationship with God, certain traditional categories—hell, purgatory, heaven—need to be restated. What of hell? Nearly all Christians today have found it important to reject the idea of a hell where God everlastingly punishes the wicked without the hope of deliverance. They have needed to reject this because a god who behaves in such a way would not be God at all, for his mercy and compassion would be sub-human. Penologists would not dream of behaving in such a way. Much less can man expect it of the all-loving God. They cannot accept that retributive justice is the ultimate law of the spiritual universe. Retribution and punishment in our society have, ideally at least, given way (and surely this is not just a passing cultural fashion?) to rehabilitation and reform. Our understanding of God as somehow more enlightened than we could ever be has caused us to change our view of the way he reacts to evil.

Traditional Christian theology has made a good deal of the contrast between *poena damni* and *poena sensus.* Pain of the senses, chiefly the eternal fire, seem unbelievably barbaric, even simply as mythological symbols. For that reason the doctrine of hell is defended today almost exclusively in terms of *poena damni,* pain of loss. It is sometimes regarded as a form of annihilation—the ultimate 'No' by or to God that brings life to an end. Yet even 'annihilation' is too strong a term for many who prefer to use the idea of 'nothingness', a negative existence, a kind of nightmare that feels endless, but which cannot be eternal, for God in his love can intervene or at least can wait patiently. If it is a condition of nothingness, there can be within it no growth or development, and therefore no hope of escape. Only the action of God can win through and transform the situation. Hell can of course be an experience of the life of this world as well as of future life, and one manifestation of it would certainly seem to be this powerlessness to act, this movement, whether a gradual drifting or a sudden falling, into a sort of paralysis of deadness from which rescue is needed. Such a view implies that nothingness need not mean annihilation. Annihilation is an irreversible process and would be quite contrary to what God intends if desire to rescue and save is in his nature.

But, equally, hell is seen as the condition in which man is almost at war with God. There is a certain sort of refusal to accept God's invitation to fellowship with him that amounts to resistance, because man has no wish to be drawn into the life of God where evil is done away and all is changed. To resist the eternal good with the only weapon appropriate, the force of evil, is an experience of hell, a battle against selfhood, a rejection of man's true destiny. That too is hell, and there could be many more descriptive pictures. Hell is not a place. It is a symbol for that state of mind where man is thoroughly off course, and such a state may take one of many forms. If after life is seen in terms of growth, almost as a journey or pilgrimage, hell is a figurative term for those who have come off the road, or have taken a route off to left or right that leads to a dead end, or, most dramatically and therefore most 'hellishly', those going in the opposite direction from that intended for them. Something is so fundamentally wrong in all these cases that growth is simply not enough—a complete change of direction or a fresh start are needed, and that requires fairly direct prompting from God. Believing in a God of rehabilitation, rather than of retribution, the Christian is confident that that prompting will not be long delayed. At death man faces judgement, not perhaps a final judgement, but a glimpse of God that throws light on his own life and forces him to make choices. The wrong choice, or perhaps more likely the refusal to accept the only viable option, leads to 'hell'. But just as life on earth has its 'hells' and its 'heavens' and a good deal of time when neither description fits well what life feels like, so, Christians may think, hell can go on being an intermittent experience beyond the grave.

What then of purgatory or 'the intermediate state' as some Anglican traditions have called it? There has always been a need felt for some such doctrine, though seldom much satisfaction with what has been contrived. Paul Tillich set out the dissatisfaction thus:

> Purgatory is a state in which the soul is 'purged' from the distorting elements of temporal existence. In Catholic doctrine, mere suffering does the purging. Besides the psychological impossibility of imagining uninterrupted periods of mere suffering, it is a theological mistake to derive transformation from pain alone instead of from grace which gives blessedness within pain . . . Protestantism was not able to answer satisfactorily the problem which originally led to the symbol of purgatory. Only one attempt, and that a rather weak one, was made to solve the problem of individual development after death (except for rare ideas of reincarnation); that doctrine was the doctrine of the intermediary state between death and resurrection (in the day of consummation). The main weakness of this doctrine is the idea of a bodiless intermediary state which contradicts the truth of the multi-dimensional unity of life and involves an unsymbolic application of measurable time to life beyond death.[17]

He might have added that the concept of 'waiting' in the Protestant intermediate state was also as inadequate as that of 'purging' in the Roman purgatory. The use of the language of growth and development is far more helpful. New growth is never a painless process and it would therefore be quite wrong to rule out all idea of pain in after life. Equally, a life of nothing but pain can be annihilating of the personality. Purgatory was traditionally regarded as the place where those who were to be saved underwent further treatment necessary before they were fit to enter God's presence. But today we can say no more than this: that purgatory is a way of speaking of the condition of those departed men and women who are going in the right direction but who still have obstacles to overcome. Unlike the souls in 'hell', there is no need for a dramatic change of course, simply a perseverance and a patience. Both purging and waiting are part of it, but neither is as important as growing. To use once again the analogy of the journey, there are the souls who are on the right road but who have not yet seen the destination.

So what of heaven? Heaven is the grasp of perfection granted to those who have made the final choice. We can believe that some come so close to selfhood, and thus to sharing in godhood, that they both see God in a way that others do not and also avoid the anxieties and sufferings that arise from uncertainty and inadequacy. To say that they are perfect is to appear to eliminate room for further development, and so we do better to speak of 'having a grasp of perfection'. It is theirs, but not wholly so. The incompleteness of their life is inevitable while there are those still further back on the journey, or even struggling down blind-alleys, and this incompleteness contributes to the dynamic sense of development even within the grasp of perfection. But, because there is the vision of God, there is complete trust, and, where there is complete trust, there is no anxiety. To reach this condition men and women must travel a long road whether in this life or beyond it. Whether we can envisage that final choice or judgement in so dramatic a form that suddenly there is a transformation to a new life is doubtful. Probably, in terms of growth towards selfhood and godhood, the alternatives that mean turning away recede—a gradual process—so that the move from 'paradise' or 'purgatory' to 'heaven' is not a sudden break but a milestone along the road. And milestones are sometimes not even noticed. But what will heaven be? Bishop Michael Ramsey paints a picture:

> Heaven! We know that analogies fail us, that prose can say little, that poetry and symbol are less misleading, that our conception of time and duration fail. But we know that the creator made us to

> worship him and to reflect his likeness, and heaven will be the perfection of that. The antitheses that so often disturb us will be resolved. Worship and service will be one. Activity and rest will find harmony. The triumph of achievement and the fascination of new discovery will be blended. There will be the vision of God in whom is the perfection of beauty, wisdom, and love.[18]

The picture of a journey is not a new one. Like all analogies, it is far from perfect, but its particular virtue, compared with other analogies, is that it makes clear the impossibility of seeing after life in terms of three 'states'—hell, purgatory, and heaven, compartmentalised regions of life beyond death, with all the departed conveniently consigned to one or another of the 'states', in such a way that they may be categorised as 'saints', 'faithful departed', 'damned', or whatever. The analogy of the journey puts every departed Christian who is on his way to salvation in essentially the same sort of condition. On the road there will be, so to speak, some far ahead and some lagging behind; some bounding forward, some finding it a struggle; some seeing sufficiently ahead to avoid obstacles, others being struck by them. So the picture goes. Any such view, as we have already seen, rejects 'states', such as purgatory, if by them we mean places in which people remain for a specified time. This does not deny the validity of them as symbols and emphases within the life beyond death, provided that their status as symbols, and symbols only, is not forgotten. We recognise that the peace and assurance of those at the end of the journey, within grasp of perfection, constitutes a higher quality of life than that of those who follow behind still touched by doubts and pains, but we rightly refuse to define a particular point at which the one changes to the other.

How do the saints fit into such a view? If the Church today is able to recover the perspective of the early Church, there is no problem. The early Christian centuries did not recognise the distinctions between saints and other Christian dead that later ages developed. In later centuries there were individuals, as we have seen, who recaptured the view of the early Church and, for all its imperfections, the *Book of Common Prayer* of 1662 did so too. The tendency to categorise the dead only developed gradually in the late patristic period, was built upon in the Middle Ages, and, for Anglicans, was given a considerable boost by the revision of 1928.

Something more needs to be said about the *imcompleteness* of the communion of saints. John Baillie poses a question:

> Even here and now (so it has come to be felt) I as an individual in the presence of God, *solus cum solo,* may begin to live the eternal life of the Heavenly Kingdom; and after release from this present life I shall enter into the fullness of its joy; and yet can my joy be full, while perhaps my friends still live on earth and I am separated from them, while our human society lives a broken and divided life, while the company of the redeemed remains incomplete? The Christian Church has steadily replied that it cannot. Its teaching, both Roman and Protestant, has been that *there can be no complete consummation for the individual until there is consummation also for society.* (his italics)[19]

This is an important insight, for Christianity of all religions stresses that a man cannot be saved alone. Because his growth to maturity is brought about not only by his relationship with God but with his fellow human beings (both his happy and his unhappy encounters with them), because indeed he is who he is chiefly because of what relationships have made him, there is a radical incompleteness about a scheme of things in which society remains divided; not of course that this insight binds us to the belief that no personality can come to the last judgement, or decision, until all can do so. All talk of time in relation to eternity is dangerous almost to the point of foolishness, but any so detailed account of how things will be is more foolish still. We do not know. But we may reasonably believe that even if there are souls who have passed the final choice there is an incompleteness when this is not shared by all.

Although it is true that in speaking of incompleteness we are emphasising that because of sin or ignorance there is a flaw in the life of the communion of saints whereby we are 'in the dark', so to speak, about the condition of most of our fellow members of the fellowship, the very fact that 'only in company with us should they reach their perfection'[20] affirms that the Church departed and the Church on earth are meant to come together. Talk of the salvation of the whole of society is talk of the communion of saints. The very fact of this radical incompleteness indicates that we are supposed to be joined together in 'one communion and fellowship'. And so what appears at first a negative point, incompleteness, turns out to be making a very positive affirmation about the way things are to grow.

A recent Anglican report[21] raises also the question of those who have died without faith, and it recognises that the Church's refusal to pray for such souls is not in keeping with a modern theological view of after life. Here the report found itself—and all those who accept the general direction of theological thinking in this area find themselves—in conflict not only with particular movements and developments in the history of the Church, but with practically the whole tradition. The Church has prayed for the 'faithful departed', but never for the 'unfaithful'. Leaving aside for a moment the whole question of prayer for the dead (to which we shall return), it is clear that for the Church to consign any man to eternal death is to usurp a divine prerogative. Eternal hell is not a concept that the Church today finds helpful. If prayer for the dead is ever appropriate, it must be for souls who died without faith. They are those for whom in Christian love the living should show the most concern. But of course the Church on earth can never know the condition of any individual, and so it cannot offer particular and specific prayers for souls it believes or even suspects are in a hell from which God must rescue them. It cannot classify the dead into faithful and unfaithful and then pray for them separately. To do so would be to make a claim to knowledge both of the mind of God and of the state of grace of the dead that could not be substantiated. So, in the same way that the Church cannot 'hive off' one section of the dead as 'saints' in a special category, so it cannot do the same with another section, the 'unfaithful'. That is just what it has done for centuries, though in its pastoral liturgy it has practiced, often unconsciously, a sort of compromise whereby it has used prayers designed for the 'faithful departed' when praying for those who apparently died without faith at all. Though this may have been somewhat dishonest, the alternative, to refuse to pray for any whose faith was suspect, would have been worse. All the departed are in God's merciful keeping. If any of them should be prayed for, so should they all.

The saints, unlike the remainder of the dead, have been said traditionally to be in 'perfect bliss'. What precisely is meant by 'bliss' or 'perfect bliss' it is difficult to be sure. The biblical language prefers to speak of 'knowledge' and perhaps perfect bliss means complete knowledge both of a purged self and of the all-holy God. But such bliss is possible only in relation to others. Until all can together achieve perfection, even those nearest to God, the 'saints', are not in a state of such perfection that they have ceased to grow. If they are still growing and moving forward, they are as likely to welcome the prayers of their fellow Christian travellers as any other group. This goes against a view already developing in the patristic age that some saints were too near to God to need our prayers. It seemed inappropriate to offer them for beings so far advanced of those on earth; especially of course was this so of the martyrs, and not only because it seemed rather forward on the part of the living, but also because of the martyrs' unique status as those who had given themselves wholeheartedly to God and had been rewarded by being admitted without delay into the joy of heaven. But if prayer for the dead is seen chiefly as an expression of love within the Christian fellowship, such loving prayer will naturally extend to the great heroes of the faith.

## V

Prayer for the dead has long been a source of conflict in the Church. Although, as we have seen, it has had a place in Christian worship from very early times, Christians in the Reformed tradition have often objected to it on the grounds that it comes too late. Death is the moment of decision and judgement. The evil go then to hell, the good either to heaven or on to a course that will lead them there in the end. Catholic orthodoxy and mainstream Anglicanism today do not subscribe to such a view. Questions of after life do leave room for both doubt and hope because of their uncertainty, and at very least we would want to express our doubt and our hope to God in prayer.

Nevertheless prayer for the dead does present problems, though not those of the traditional Protestant objections. The first we have touched on already. It is the question of the appropriateness of the language employed in such prayer. We have already noted part of this prayer used until recently in the Roman Church:

> O Lord Jesus Christ, King of glory, deliver the souls of all the faithful departed from the pains of hell and from the depths of the pit: deliver them from the lion's mouth, that hell devour them not, that they fall not into darkness . . .[22]

The idea that anyone, however evil, should be sent by the all-loving God to these tortures, however symbolic the language, seems to us inconceivable. That it should not be those without faith, but the 'faithful departed' who should have to be delivered from them is the more remarkable. But language such as this can still be heard in such Anglican churches as retain the old Roman forms (though Rome has abandoned them) and some twentieth-century Anglicans therefore still have their view of after life shaped by these harsh sentiments. Many more examples of such prayer could be given. The *Dies Irae* must suffice as one further example. It dates from the thirteenth century but can still be heard in use today.

> Lo! the book exactly worded,
> Wherein all hath been recorded;
> Thence shall judgement be awarded.
>
> When the Judge his seat attaineth,
> And each hidden deed arraigneth,
> Nothing unavenged remaineth . . .
>
> When the wicked are confounded,
> Doomed to shame and woe unbounded
> Call me, with thy Saints surrounded . . .[23]

Such words are so obviously inadequate and sub-Christian that it may be easy for most people to see them for the fine poetry, but poor theology, that they are. The more dangerous sort of prayer is perhaps the more reasonable kind that cannot be so easily dismissed. The new Anglican burial rite prays:

> Remember, O Lord, this your servant, who has gone before us with the sign of faith, and now rests in the sleep of peace. According to your promises, grant to *him* and to all who rest in Christ, refreshment, light, and peace.[24]

Here 'modern' liturgy still speaks of the dead in terms of the attainment of static rest, rather than in terms of increasing perfection. The prayer—and it is a typical one—emphasises rest, sleep, and peace, all of which seem to speak more of the *Sheol* of the Old Testament than of the great pilgrimage to the vision of God that the Christian undertakes. There is no mention of continual growth in God's love and service.

But though the question of liturgical language constitutes a problem, it is not the fundamental problem of prayer for the dead. The root problem is concerned with the whole question of intercessory prayer. This is not the place to expound a doctrine of intercessory prayer, but, though all intercessory prayer seems to raise questions in terms of precisely what we are seeking to do, prayer for the dead presents the problem in its most acute form, because of our ignorance when we pray for the dead both of those for whom we pray and also of whether we are even on the right track in presuming to pray for them. Bishop Ian Ramsey wrote:

> Intercessory prayer cannot be wholly segregated from other forms, and (potentially, at least) is a demanding occupation. It is quite improper to have prayers for (say) a war in Indo-China, for sick people, for the parishes of a diocese . . . and so on, unless the actual problems in some way or other form part of our lives—whether by work, or gifts or protest marches or by some other imaginative concern or inner identification.[25]

The problem of the dead cannot form part of our lives in the way that wars or sick people or churches can because we cannot act. We cannot really even enter into imaginative concern or make some inner identification, for we have no reliable data to go on. Our prayer is entirely in the dark. Can we pray effectively when we do not know enough detail about the situation involved to specify what changes in it would be desirable? If we cannot, then prayer for the dead will fail to achieve what it set out to do. If, however, simply to name the departed before the all-loving God, knowing that he will do what is best, is enough, then ignorance is no great obstacle.

Nevertheless the doubt remains. What do Christians think they are doing in praying for the dead? The Doctrine Commission's report of 1971 articulated the worries we ought to feel:

> When we are praying for the departed, are we asking God to do things he has already determined either to do or not to do, so that our prayer can have no effect upon the issue one way or another? Are we asking God to change his mind as to the fate of, or the treatment in store for, particular souls? Are we assuming that, in default of our prayers, God will not do the good things for which we are asking? Or that unless we pray he will not do these good things as effectively or quickly, so that our prayers have power to intensify or speed up God's action?[26]

These are fundamental questions that arise in connection with prayer for the living as much as for the dead. There is a good deal of caution among theologians about what it is appropriate to say in any intercessory prayer. Combine caution about intercessory prayer with agnosticism about the condition of the departed, and any form of prayer that is very specific, or envisages very exactly the needs of the dead, seems presumptuous.

What form are these prayers to take? There is a good argument for almost total silence, because our knowledge is so small. But, on the other hand, there is a need to spell out our hopes and fears simply because of our lack of knowledge. Men and women will pray for the dead, especially the dead to whom they have been close in this life, and the task of the Church must therefore be to provide them with words to say and ideas to articulate, which, while they may go too far for the theologian in appearing to give too much weight to speculative ideas, at least say the sort of things that do not conflict with our understanding of God and do not violate too drastically the rule of agnosticism that we have to retain in the back of our mind. Symbols and images are dangerous, but people will use symbols and images. Best they should be given the least misleading symbols and images. In the past, as we have seen, they have often employed quite inappropriate language that has implied things about God which, if they were true, would make him less than God. To caricature slightly the prayer of the Church in the past we should say that it prayed for the dead, seeking for them both deliverance from hell through the merits of Christ's death and also rest and peace, and gave thanks for the saints, not presuming to pray for them but seeking their prayers and grace to imitate them. Not all these sentiments are by any means wrong, but, while other things remain unsaid, there is an unbalanced and distorted picture of Christian eschatology. How is this to be rectified? The Anglican Doctrine Commission's report of 1971 proposed a number of prayers that fitted well with the sort of theological position it had reached. The prayer in the section on 'Prayer for the Christian Dead' reads:

> May God in his infinite love and mercy bring the whole Church, living and departed in the Lord Jesus, to a joyful resurrection and the fulfilment of his eternal kingdom.

That in the section on 'Prayer for the Non-Christian Dead' reads:

> O God of infinite mercy and justice, who hast made men in thine own image, and hatest nothing that thou hast made, we rejoice in thy love for all creation and commend all men to thee, that in them thy will be done, in and through Jesus Christ our Lord.

And, finally, the section entitled 'The Prayers of the Christian Dead' concludes with the words:

> We thank you, O God, for your grace revealed in all the Saints, and we pray for faith and courage, hope and love like theirs, through their example and in fellowship with them, through Jesus Christ our Lord.[27]

Looked at as a whole these prayers include most of the ideas about after life that we could possibly want to find included. The first idea is to emphasise that all the dead are to be considered together—'bring the whole Church, living and departed'; 'we rejoice in thy love for all creation and commend all men to thee'. Though sometimes we shall want to single out the great heroes of faith for particular mention, we shall never want to pray for the dead in such a way that we seem to exclude either the saints, as not in the same need as others, or the non-Christian dead, as beyond God's love.

The second idea is to introduce right at the beginning a clear acknowledgement that we can pray very little with certainty. We do not know the exact condition or needs of the dead. We therefore express our trust in God and our belief that he will do what he alone can know needs doing. Such an agnosticism is marked by the use of the word 'commend' in which all is left to God as we simply express a concern—'we commend all men to thee, that in them thy will be done'.

Thirdly, such prayer should include some reference to sin and forgiveness, perhaps mentioning the significance in this connection of the death of Jesus or his cross. Though we shall want to avoid the excessive hell-fire language of the past, an expression of trust in God's forgiveness is important if the prayer is not to drift into a sort of easy and unconditional immortality doctrine. So we make reference to God's 'infinite mercy and justice' and remind ourselves that he 'hateth nothing' that he has made. We could argue quite reasonably that none of the prayers reproduced above contains this element with enough force. Indeed it is quite lacking in two of them. Perhaps they reveal that the pendulum could swing too far away from the old obsession with the fire of hell and eternal death to something with no element of judgement in it at all.

A fourth element present is an acknowledgement of the special impact of the lives of the great saints. We shall want to find at least an expression of thankfulness for their witness to God's power in their lives (or, less suitably, for their example) and of the encouragement it gives us. But we shall not want such prayer to over-emphasise the distinction between them and the rest of the departed.

The fifth idea that ought to be present is the idea of mutuality. The living and the dead belong together. This will normally be expressed by use of the words 'fellowship' or 'communion' or simply by using the word 'Church' in such a context that it clearly means both the living and the dead. Sometimes we shall want to spell out that mutuality must imply that the departed are concerned with us as we are with them. We may want to mention their prayers, but we know this to be on dangerous ground and so we shall choose our words well. The three prayers above do not really do justice to this idea of mutuality, and fellowship is only mentioned in the prayer specifically concerned with the great heroes of faith.

A sixth element is mention of the resurrection. In the past prayer has tended to emphasise the connection between Christian death and the death of Christ, but it is a wise modern perspective that wants to associate the continued aliveness of the departed with the resurrection life of Christ, who is the first of many brothers, as Paul did. Thus the first prayer asks that the Church may be brought to 'a joyful resurrection'. This idea of resurrection is particularly apparent in the liturgy for the dead in the Roman Church; and Anglicans could learn a good deal from it about the element of joy that it so tellingly introduces into a subject in which solemnity to the point of sadness often dominates. One such Roman prayer reads:

> Merciful Father,
> hear our prayer and console us.
> As we renew our faith in your Son,
> whom you raised from the dead,
> strengthen our hope that all our departed brothers and sisters
> will share in his resurrection.[28]

The final idea explicit in the Anglican prayers already quoted is that of radical incompleteness. Prayer for the departed must include a recognition that there is a consummation still to come and that, even if some of the dead now have joy with God, there is greater joy to come. The incompleteness is because we are not yet admitted fully into fellowship with God and with them. So the prayer looks forward to 'the fulfilment of his eternal kingdom.'

But there do seem to be two rather important elements missing from the Anglican prayers. The element of rest and peace is entirely lacking. Certainly in the past it has been over-emphasised and, when so used, it has given a quite distorted and static view of life after death. Nevertheless to remove it entirely is regrettable. Death must mean for some delivery from suffering in this world. A new tranquility will set in, or so we hope. All, we trust, will know sin forgiven and that will mean a shedding of anxiety and fear, that must result in peace of mind. Thought of peace and rest should therefore be retained, though not in the supreme position it once occupied. The other element missing is that quite central one of growth and development in service and knowledge of God beyond death, of which so much has already been said that no more need be added. Its omission from the forms reproduced is very regrettable and renders them all less than satisfactory.

The modern Roman Catholic prayers reveal a slightly different picture and a less radical one. The saints and the rest of the departed remain two quite distinct categories. The fellowship of the saints is strongly underlined, but their witness and the encouragement it gives are hardly mentioned. Our solidarity with the Church departed and our hope with them of the resurrection are the dominant themes.

## vi

Laying aside the question of how the saints should be honoured, whether by prayers, feast days, or whatever, it is important to examine by what criteria the Church today is to single out particular men and women as heroes of the faith. We have noted how the Church of the past has done it, but do the considerations of modern theology outlined here necessitate a modification of these criteria?

Traditionally the Church has expected of its canonised saints above all else orthodoxy of belief, else the name of Clement of Alexandria would not have been excised from early martyrologies by Clement VIII on the grounds of the doubtful orthodoxy of his writings.[29] Such an attitude reflects a narrow view of the nature of faith. It sees faith as an assent to a series of doctrinal propositions rather than as a trusting response to God. But it is difficult to begin to test whether a man is a man of faith except by reference to what he has said about doctrinal propositions, for the nature of his response to God in any more personal way is not likely to be a matter of public knowledge. What is certain is that the Roman Catholic Church has canonised men and women whose doctrinal views were sufficiently divergent to be regarded as virtual opposites. Once we realise that only an artificial synthesis can produce a non-negotiable form of the faith, then we have to recognise that saints, as much as any other Christians, will have expressed their belief in God in different ways, and we shall not seek a rigid orthodoxy. This does not mean that anybody, whatever his views, can be regarded as a saint. That would only be the case if orthodoxy were the only criterion.

In the past, heresy was very much on a par with schism as offences which barred a man or woman from recognition as a saint. There was a good deal to be said for such a view. The Church was right to regard the perpetrators of schism as men who had brought great harm to the community in destroying the unity of its fellowship. Trying to see things as those within the Church saw them then, we may well sympathise with the view that, however corrupt or ineffective the Church may become, it is the task of those within it to remain within to fight the inadequacies and evils they discern. The scandal of the Church's inadequacy is in no way removed by the scandal of its disunity. So the argument would run; and it is clearly not one that can be lightly dismissed. And it is possible to go further. Can it make any logical sense at all to regard as a brother, and even an exalted and glorified brother, one who when he was alive chose to reject the brotherhood? Can we see as a prime figure in the communion of saints one who chose to be out of communion in this life? It is such a view that has led, quite logically, the Roman Church to give no recognition at all to schismatics, the Anglican Church not to recognise post-Reformation Roman saints (Anglicanism here regarding itself as the Catholic Church in England and the Roman Church as an imposter destroying the unity, just as a schismatic does) and present-day Anglicans to throw up their hands in horror that men like John Wesley and George Fox should receive calendrical recognition in the Church of England. The key to a reconsideration of such a view lies in our concept of the Church. It is becoming increasingly clear to Christian denominations, including the Roman Church, that no particular church or sect can claim a monopoly of truth, and indeed that within all main stream Christian groupings God is seen at work, and his power is manifested in heroic and holy people. Especially when talking of the saints of recent times, it is folly to disregard men like Dietrich Bonhoeffer or Martin

Luther-King simply because from birth they had been brought up in a Reformed non-episcopal tradition.

That members of other Christian denominations are to be regarded as saints is probably not a matter of much controversy today, but there would be those who, accepting that especially of people born into existing separated churches or sects, would doubt whether those who actually brought about the divisions should be so recognised. Is not the breaking of his body too serious a crime against Christ to be easily set aside? Three comments must be made on this view. Firstly it is very rare for the fault to be on one side only in any dispute of the type that leads to separation in the Church. For instance, it is possible to maintain that Martin Luther-King was no more responsible for the Reformation divisions than those whose corruption he fought. Was not division within the church the inevitable outcome of a history where folly after folly gradually built up an explosive situation where only something dramatic could resolve tension? Secondly, it ought to be possible for Christians to recognise such imperfections and indeed sin within their own church that it might be the will of God to purge these by division. For it is not reasonable to make of disunity a sort of ultimate sin against the Holy Spirit. Those who most loudly condemn schism are often also the strongest exponents of the need always to be upholding truth. Time and time again in the history of the church, the cause of unity and the cause of truth have seemed, so far as men could see, to be on the sort of collision course where one must give way to the other. Those who chose truth, as they saw it, were as likely to be upholding the honour of the Spirit of truth as insulting the Spirit of unity.

Thirdly (and this leads into the next general attribute we need to examine) the action of those who appear to promote division must be looked at in terms of their integrity. Did they honestly believe themselves to be doing God's will? Were they trying to conform to the divine plan? If they were, they were men of integrity and as such they were in a right relationship with God. It is no contradiction to maintain that a man could be wrong about an issue and yet in a right relationship with God. And Christian sanctity belongs to the man in the right relationship rather than to the man with the right views. It is because of this emphasis on integrity that a calendar of saints can include two men who very fundamentally disagreed. Sometimes it is clear to us, in the light of history, which was right. Sometimes it is not.

But even where it is, we are not by that prevented from honouring as a saint the one who was wrong, providing that his relationship with God was a right one. It is this attitude which allows us to consider the inclusion in the calendar of both Thomas Cranmer and Thomas More. The same attitude allowed the English church to recognise as saints both Wilfrid and Chad, who did not see eye to eye at all.

What then is required beyond integrity and faith (by which is meant a living relationship with God, the father of Jesus Christ, rather than assent to a set of propositions)? Very little else is required in every saint. But a little more must be said about this 'faith' of which we have thought already. It does not need to be an ostentatious and loud proclamation of God's love. Nevertheless there has to have been about the life of the saint an attractiveness, a sort of magnetic pull, that made people feel that here was a life lived close to God—increasingly close as it went on—and one through which God could disclose himself. It is difficult to define it more than that, for what form that characteristic would take would vary considerably. It would however usually be of such a type that men could see that the life had direction towards God, could feel that the life had dependence on God and was lived in the knowledge that it was the life of a sinner in need of the divine forgiveness. For holiness has never been well defined as 'being good'. It is about wanting to be good. But chiefly it is about knowing oneself to be evil, but forgiven. So there is about the life of the authentic saint some indication of his awareness of his own poverty of spirit. We have described the saints as witnesses to God. The true saint certainly knows that anything in his life that seems good and positive is not by his own effort but by God's grace. So his sanctity does not reflect his goodness, but witnesses to God's.

Other than that, the mark of the communion of saints will be variety. There is no such thing as a stereotyped Christian saint. Men and women of faith and integrity will be of many different kinds and this variety is a great richness in the life of the Church. Some will have been people of outstanding intellectual ability who helped the Church to a more helpful understanding of God; others will have been outstanding exponents of prayer and spirituality, others zealous reformers of Church or society, others quiet unassuming servants of God whose inner holiness shone through apparently insignificant lives. Some will be those who died for the faith. What are we to make of that in the light of what was said about modern western society's attitude to the death of the hero, eventually regarding it as defeat rather than victory?[30] This is a case where we must be careful not simply to assimilate society's view and to accept it as inevitable. For, if the church stands for anything at all, it stands for the belief that out of apparent defeat and failure comes hope and life. The Church's view stands over and against the world's. If it cannot portray the death of its great ones as the triumphs it believes them to be—truimphs of faith, endurance, trust, and sacrifice—then it has no hope at all of convincing the world of the significance and lordship of its greatest martyr, Jesus. Not only then must the Church retain its belief in the value of martyrdom, but must require of all its saints that there be something of the martyr in their attitude to life. That will be so because true faith, the mark of the saint, remains confident in the face of death, and integrity requires endurance to the point of death.

What is to be said about the blemishes in the lives of the saints? Even among the canonised saints there are no shortage of people with whom life would have been distinctly uncomfortable. Donald Attwater writes, for instance, of Saint Jerome that he was

> in some ways a contradictory character. His religious ideals were pitched very high; he held the affection of his friends and followers; he was considerate to the weak and lowly. On the other hand there were his intemperateness in controversy, his contempt for opponents, the virulence of his tongue and pen, his savage and insulting invective. To attribute these things simply to too close a following of classical rhetorical models is perhaps a little naive. The remark attributed to Pope Sixtus V seems more to the point: looking at a picture which showed Jerome beating his breast with a stone, Sixtus is said to have observed, 'You do well thus to use that stone: without it you would never have been numbered among the saints.[31]

Many of the saints displayed characteristics not much less objectionable than Jerome's. But the words attributed, whether apocryphal or not, to Pope Sixtus get to the heart of the matter. The saint is the penitent, the man who knows his sin and seeks the forgiveness of God. Our modern view of after life in terms of growth and development has had a liberating effect on what we have to say about the blemishes in the lives of the saints. For, if we believe that, even for the greatest of saints, there is growth in self-knowledge and in both knowledge and love of God to follow after death as well as before it, we become less concerned to find in the life of the saint perfection of living. Instead we are content to discern the right direction in movement towards God. Because we feel this need only to discern direction, rather than perfection, we are less concerned to idealise the saints. We are happier to present them 'warts and all'. This represents not so much a lowering of standards but a more honest presentation of them. It so happens that it also makes the saints more attractive to a generation that has little interest in heroes 'ten foot tall'.

## vii

The whole tenor of what has gone before has been to play down any distinction between the saints and the remainder of the dead. And this, as we have seen,[32] is not a particularly novel idea but finds expression in the *Book of Common Prayer* of 1662. What bearing does that insight have on the observance of All Saints' Day and All Souls' Day, which are observed on the first two days of November? The logical outcome of this ancient (and restored) theological outlook would be the abolition of All Souls' Day, in order that all the great truths of the communion of saints can be seen together in the celebration of the one great feast in which no one aspect of the doctrine receives undue attention to the detriment of others. And, if the Church chose to do that, it would be understandable. Nevertheless a word of caution may be sounded. All Saints' Day is rightly marked by great joy and festivity as the Church on earth reminds itself of its solidarity today with the church beyond the grave and its confident faith that that solidarity will merge into unity. On such a day the elements of sin and forgiveness tend to find little expression. But there is a need to acknowledge that the dead have died imperfect and have needed to come to God in penitence, trusting his goodness and love whereby they can receive forgiveness. Death is about judgement, whatever else it may be. And the liturgy of the Church must meet man's emotional need to express his anxiety about the dead, especially those who have in no obvious sense lived by faith or died in it. All Souls' Day, with its stark recollection of man's sin and need of divine forgiveness, is a telling response to that need. There may therefore be a case for continuing to observe at All Saints'-tide a day when these particular elements of what we believe about life after death are given particular weight. But, if that is so, then the liturgy of the day needs to express these elements with care. There are few occasions in the year where the present liturgical practice fails more sadly to meet the theological standards required.

# 8 *Sanctity and Recognition*

## i

In its 1976 report,[1] The Church of England Liturgical Commission acknowledges the problems involved in observing adequately the feast days of the Church.

> In framing the calendar, we have tried to take account of the devotional needs of the Church of England and the realities of the contemporary situation. The Book of Common Prayer provides a table 'of all the feasts *that are to be observed* in the Church of England'. It begins with 'All Sundays in the year', and continues with the days which we know as Red Letter days, setting the saints' days (not to mention the Monday and Tuesday in Easter Week and Whitweek) on a level with Sunday, and claiming that they are days when the faithful members of the Church should acknowledge a duty to attend a service. The modern reality in very many parishes is that no attempt is made to provide services on Red Letter days, and the pastor may well prefer to concentrate his attention on proclaiming the duty of worship on Sundays, and a few other major festivals.[2]

Such a situation calls into question the whole idea of saints' days. For most church-going people in the late twentieth century, public worship means an hour on Sunday morning and no more, except on a very rare weekday, such as Christmas or Good Friday. Of course there are places and conditions where this does not apply. Various communities, colleges, and institutions are able to maintain daily worship in which a significant proportion of the community participates. In some parish churches more than a handful of faithful people are sometimes present at a weekday celebration of the Eucharist, but this is the exception rather than the rule. There would seem to be a case for an observance on a Sunday of some of those major themes, events, and heroes that in the past have usually fallen on a weekday. The Commission appears to have been working in this direction when it ensured that certain themes—the Conversion of Paul, the Charge to Peter, the Annunciation to Mary—found a place in the Sunday cycle of lections. But it did not take the process very far. To take but one example: The Feast of the Epiphany is one of the days that is by common agreement a festival that deserves full observance in the Church and yet which fails to receive it unless 6 January falls on a Sunday. We should therefore expect the Commission to allocate a Sunday to its observance. It does do so, but chooses the Second Sunday after Christmas, which is a Sunday that occurs only in certain years, and then alternates the Epiphany theme with that of the visit to Jerusalem of the twelve year old Jesus.[3] In practice therefore the Epiphany theme will receive adequate treatment in one year in, say, four. Among the saints only Mary, the mother of the Lord[4] (Advent 4), St. John Baptist (Advent 3), and the Conversion of St. Paul (Epiphany 2) receive any very full observance on a Sunday every year, though St. Peter in Year 1 of the two year cycle forms a major part of the subject matter on two Sundays, Lent 3 (when the gospel is the Caesarea Philippi incident)[5] and Easter 4 (when the gospel is the Charge to Peter)[6]. In year 2, however, Peter receives no attention.

The Commission could have taken this process to its logical conclusion and *substituted* Sunday observance for the traditional dates of a number of feasts. Instead it chooses to leave the traditional dates unaltered in addition to the new observance within the Sunday cycle, a confusing duplication. If agreement could be reached ecumenically about new Sunday dates for feasts, there would be great benefit in abandoning traditional commemorations. The movement in the Roman Church has been against the intrusion into the liturgical year of commemorations of saints, but these proposals would not constitute intrusions, since they would be introduced at the appropriate points in the unfolding of the liturgical cycle—the Annunciation in Advent, St. Peter in Eastertide, for instance. The new lectionary points to developments along these lines.

A word must be said about festivals of the Blessed Virgin Mary. The *Book of Common Prayer* orders the celebration of the Feast of the Presentation of Christ in the Temple (which it subtitles 'The Purification of St. Mary the Virgin') and the Prayer Book emphasis on this being a feast of our Lord, not of his mother, has rightly returned in current thinking. If the Sunday lectionary were sensibly reordered, this feast would move from 2 February to an appropriate Sunday, possibly the last Sunday after Epiphany, if the feast is to retain its old sense of bringing to a final close the celebration of Christmas. In any case, it is not chiefly a feast of Mary. The Prayer Book also orders 'The Annunciation of the Blessed Virgin Mary' on 25 March, nine months before Christmas Day. Again, such a feast could well be removed from the calendar since it is observed on Advent 3. Furthermore, like the Presentation, this is not chiefly a feast of our Lady. Several new calendars designate it 'The Annunciation *of Our Lord* to the Blessed Virgin Mary'.[7] The Prayer Book calendar names, but makes no liturgical provision for, 'The Visitation of the Blessed Virgin Mary' on 2 July. The observance of this day is appropriate, for it is an attractive biblical incident, though probably not one that needs Sunday observance. If distinctions between different categories of observance are to be retained, it probably does not merit *red letter* status. 8 September is named 'The Nativity of the Blessed Virgin Mary'. There is of course no biblical account of this event. Were there no more appropriate occasion to celebrate the mother of the Lord, the birth would be a suitable occasion. But, given that there are more suitable dates, this particular observance seems a little superfluous. The final Prayer Book date is 8 December, 'The Conception of the Blessed Virgin Mary'. It is difficult to see why this particular event should call for liturgical commemoration, except of course where a doctrine of immaculate conception is held. Where such a belief is not current, the feast loses all point and modern Anglican revisions have sensibly omitted it.

Neither the Prayer Book, nor the revision of 1928, makes mention of the traditional feast of Mary on 15 August. By 1969, Anglican liturgists were considering the matter:

> Two entries in particular have exercised the mind of the Commission. One is the Falling Asleep of the Blessed Virgin Mary, which we have not included in our proposals ... We would point out that this appears in many calendars of the Anglican Communion, and that to observe it does not commit us to a doctrine of the corporal assumption; moreover the date on which a saint is normally commemorated is the date of his or her death. On the other hand the calendar already contains the traditional commemoration of the birth, the annunciation, and the visitation of the Blessed Virgin Mary.[8]

Since 1969, however, there has been more than one change of mind. Partly because of a lowering of the level of suspicion by the Evangelical party, but also because of the happy solution of the American Episcopal Church to the problem of what title[9] to give to the festival, the Commission in 1976 felt able to recommend that 15 August be observed as the Festival of the Blessed Virgin Mary. The Commission justified its recommendation thus:

> A festival of the Blessed Virgin on this date was first observed by the eastern Church in the early seventh century and was adopted by the western Church about a century later. It originally commemorated the death, as other saints' days commemorate the death of other saints, but later became associated under a variety of titles with doctrines which are not regarded as part of the Church of England's doctrine. However, the Festival of the Annunciation is widely regarded as a festival of our Lord and not of our Lady, and upon this understanding of the matter it follows that the Church of England has no festival devoted to the Blessed Virgin herself. These considerations led us to agree that there ought to be a festival devoted to the Blessed Virgin Mary, in her own right so to speak, and one which related to the whole of her life, and not simply to some incident in it: and on the other hand that the title of such a festival ought to give no countenance to any unacceptable doctrine. Our agreement on these principles led us to agree further that a festival of the Blessed Virgin Mary on August 15 would be a desirable enrichment of our calendar and one which accorded with the Church's best traditions.[10]

The Commission therefore proposed that 15 August be kept as a greater holy day. The Visitation (renamed 'the Visit') was to be kept on the new Roman date of 31 May as a 'lesser festival'. The Nativity and the Conception did not appear in the calendar. The Commission was right that a date should be given to the recalling of Mary in the totality of her life, obedience, and witness. This is a different exercise from the recalling of the Annunciation. The difficulty with 15 August is that it falls in the middle of a holiday period when it is more difficult than usual to ensure adequate liturgical observance. But the great strength of the date is its ecumenical value. The figure of Mary has been the centre of much controversy in the Church and the celebration by all the historic Christian churches of a feast in her honour on one and the same day is a powerful symbol of growing together and unity.

In February 1978 the General Synod the Church of England made a number of alterations to the proposals of its own Revision Committee. The Feast of the Blessed Virgin Mary was the principal change. The Synod decided to abandon the idea of restoring 15 August to the English calendar and opted instead for 8 September, traditionally the Feast of the *Nativity* of the

Blessed Virgin. Subsequent revisers may think this decision was a hasty and unfortunate one, for the Church of England will now celebrate its principal feast of the mother of the Lord on a different date from the majority of Christendom.

The celebration of the saints of God is principally not a matter of naming individuals and recalling singular acts or lives of heroism. It is above all a rejoicing within a communion or fellowship.[11] The celebration of All Saints' Day, the day on which this great credal affirmation is emphasised, should be widespread and as near as possible to what a more rigorist age called a 'feast of obligation'. The problem of weekday observance raises itself again. Anticipating this problem and proposing half a solution to it, the Liturgical Commission gives to the last Sunday before the Fifth Sunday before Advent the theme of 'Citizens of Heaven'. The All Saints' Day theme has therefore been built into the Sunday cycle, though without its name and without much of a feeling of festival. The choice of day is of course highly appropriate. It is the obvious theme with which to conclude the cycle. In that respect the Commission is right. But if it is to be well celebrated, and if unnecessary repetition is to be avoided only about a fortnight later, should not the Commission have considered renaming this Sunday 'All Saints' Day' with 1 November losing that designation? It would be a radical move and the Commission was possibly right not to make it, but the matter is at least worthy of discussion and ecumenical consultation.

If, in some future revision of the calendar, it could be ensured that the whole communion of saints in general, and the great saints in particular, were recognised and celebrated on Sundays, would the need for saints' days disappear? Theologically, we have already noted,[12] there is an argument against singling out individuals, both because it gives a wrong emphasis in an area where the social nature of the fellowship of all believers is what really matters, and also because the commemoration of one individual tends to mark him out as an *example*, where the total impact of the communion of saints is one of *witness*. The naming of individuals among the saints is but the first step on a path that can lead a person to believe in the ability to communicate personally with departed individuals and to experiment in all sorts of inadvisable spiritualist practices. And yet, valid as all that is, the contrary arguments have usually, and rightly, prevailed. Of these, the principal argument is a very old one.

The early Christians were encouraged, at a time of persecution and challenge, by the witness of those in whose lives there had been such heroism, holiness, single-mindedness, and love that they had overcome in life, and sometimes in death, all that challenged and threatened. Most of these whom they venerated were not distant figures of the past, but men and women whom they had themselves known or who belonged to the relatively recent past. The Church in our own day is beset with problems and challenges on every side. It has, to some extent, lost its confidence. The witness of its ancient heroes, but especially its more modern heroes, can be a source of inspiration to it. In particular the parish priest who gathers around him a small congregation of faithful people to celebrate the Eucharist, or even more the parish priest who goes into his church each day to say his office quite alone, can be encouraged by calling to mind Christian saints who have lived and worshipped and worked in like circumstances and who are united with him in the prayer he offers each day.

Another reason for giving time to the recalling of the heroes of the past lies in the peculiar circumstances of the age in which we live. It is the era of the 'New Reformation' in which much that the Church has treasured, often without much thought, has been jettisoned in the interest of responding to the demands of a new age. Such radical reform has clearly been necessary and the work of the Holy Spirit is discerned within it. But the faithfulness and piety of men and women of the past, and their ability to find, worship, and respond to the living God within the structures that are now being dismantled, serves to make the Church hesitate before plunging too enthusiastically into every reform; and that can be no bad thing.

We noted that one of the reasons for increased calendrical observance of the saints in the last one hundred years was the increase of daily worship, especially of the daily Eucharist, and the need to bring into that a variety that the daily repetition of the Sunday propers could never give. The same argument still remains, though it has been weakened by the introduction of the Sunday themes and richer seasonal material and propers. Where a calendar is overloaded with a host of obscure saints their commemoration can mean very little, but the occasional day given over to the commemoration of an intelligible figure about whom a good deal can be known, can give to a week just that change and variety that is needed if the weekly theme is not to wear very thin as it is carried on from day to day. This will apply above all in those places where a community of people meet daily, or almost daily, to celebrate the Eucharist; and there is no doubt that the Church of England has failed in the past to make adequate liturgical provision in this respect for colleges, institutions, and other communities. But it will apply also to the priest (or lay person) saying the morning or evening office in private. There is a widespread failure by the clergy to say their daily office. In part this could be because of its lack of variety and colour. There is also a growing tendency among Anglican clergy to use the new Roman office, presumably because it is rich in just the respects in which its Anglican counterpart is poor.

It follows from this that where a saint is to be commemorated there should be adequate and rich liturgical provision for this. Although the Prayer Book of 1928 and the recent General Synod legislation go much further than the *Book of Common Prayer* in providing at least collect and lections for all days, there is a need to go much further than this. First of all there is a need to provide a greater variety of collects, psalmody, and lections. For instance, in following the 1978 proposals for the calendar, one could use the collect for a teacher of the faith or confessor four times in seventeen days—on the festivals of St. Hilary, St. Francis of Sales, St. John Chrysostom, and St. Thomas Aquinas. But, most important, there is a need to provide suitable scriptural sentences and antiphons, biographical material written for liturgical reading, extracts, where appropriate, from the writings of the saint, and suggested intercessory material arising from aspects of his life and work. There is also a need to find a way by which, without abandoning entirely the regular and systematic reading of the scriptures and recitation of the psalms, the observance of the festival can be made a reality in the daily office as well as in the Eucharist. This would be a profound enrichment to the liturgy of the Church and the spirituality of its clergy.

## ii

Having decided that there should be a calendar of the saints, it is now necessary to examine by what process a Christian man or woman should be placed in the calendar. All that we have written about life in the communion of saints would seem to throw doubt on any formal canonisation process. We have noted that within the communion of saints we all belong together and have even now a certain measure of fellowship, but one about which we can speak only in general terms. One of the implications of the radical incompleteness of things may be that even the saints live in ignorance of the details of our human condition as we are of theirs. Certainly it would be an unjustifiably bold assertion to suggest that individual saints have particular and specialised knowledge of individual living Christians on earth, in the same way that, however confident we may be about the direction in which the whole body of saints is moving, we remain quite unable to say anything exact about the particular conditions, or stage of the journey, at any given moment, of any one of the departed. The whole emphasis of talk of the communion of saints is not on our relationship with individuals, but on our participation in the totality of God's creation. Our relationship in prayer is one in which we join our prayer with that of the whole Church, living and dead, worshipping God, commending each other to his mercy, and, above all, praying for the perfection of our communion with both God and each other, without which things remain radically incomplete. In a word, we refuse to categorise the dead. There are not saints and others. We are all together on the journey to God, though not all at the same stage of the journey.

We have already noted that in the early Church the making of a saint was at first a spontaneous act of a local community.[13] But it was not long before such canonisation by acclamation was brought under control. The later half of the first millennium marked a period of increasing control by authorities—episcopal, synodical, and papal—over the process until in the twelfth century nothing less than papal approval, given after much evidence and then only if political circumstances were right, would suffice.[14] This formal process is designed to examine carefully the life of the candidate for canonisation in order to discover if it was of such a calibre that God would, in all justice, have to admit him to eternal bliss because of his great holiness. Evidence of miracles at the candidate's intercession would be sought (except in the case of martyrs) as an indication that he was indeed in a position to petition God, in other words with him in heaven. The building of formal and legal procedures on to a foundation of symbolic language is an improper exercise, and the results are unreliable. The whole canonisation process is based on a view of after life in terms of the three *states* of heaven, purgatory, and hell and the need to establish that a would-be saint is without doubt in heaven, the happy *state*. It assumes too that the radical incompleteness that denies full fellowship with all the Christian dead to us denies it also to souls in purgatory, but not to saints in heaven. Thus the saints know our needs and pray for us, whereas the remainder of the dead, being in ignorance of our condition, if they pray for us at all, do so in the same sort of ignorance of our circumstances that we have of theirs. Remove these distinctions of *state* and condition and of vision and ability to offer effective prayers (and a modern symbolic picture in terms of growth to God or a journey to God does remove them), and canonisation appears a useless exercise, seeking to find assurance of things which can never be known and to bestow status that may well not exist.

For this reason such talk in Anglican circles as in the 1957 Report,[15] which tries to decide whether this or that person, whether Charles I or Edward King, has been canonised 'by the back door', is quite irrelevant. We should not declare people saints, though we cannot but be moved by sanctity. Putting people in a calendar is quite a different matter. In doing that we simply assert that, among all the millions who are on the journey to God, these are the ones whose memories we find it helpful to reflect upon. By so doing we do not attempt to define where precisely on the road they are, though we would not include them if we did not believe they were going in the right direction. Talk in Anglican circles of reviving canonisation would best be speedily forgotten. Whether it was a rare insight, or simply an oversight, that stopped the English Reformers from making provision for canonisation we do not know. But their neglect of the subject is to our benefit!

Even where there is to be no canonisation, a fairly vigorous system of selection is needed in the drawing up of the calendar. The Church may not be looking for saints in a technical sense, but it is nevertheless seeking to hold up for veneration and edification only those heroic Christians whose lives can help draw men and women towards God. The haphazard way in which the Church of England Liturgical Commission approached the task is no way in which to make decisions such as these. Names were put into draft calendars, removed, and restored, at the whim of commission members, without any proper examination of their case or consideration of the criteria by which the calendar should be drawn up.[16] What is required is a set of guidelines both on the procedure to be adopted in bringing a name into the calendar and also on the criteria of sanctity against which a name is to be tested. Although the Church of England does well to avoid the canonisation procedures of the Roman Church, its own total lack of procedure goes too far in the opposite direction. Perhaps the most acceptable procedure would be for a name to be placed before the General Synod by a Diocesan Synod, where a diocese has already incorporated the name into its own calendar for a number of years and found the observance to be helpful to the Church. The General Synod would refer the name to a small commission which would examine the possibility of including the new name in the national calendar. If it recommended inclusion, the name would be added to the calendar not only by a vote of the synod, but by a solemn liturgical ceremony. About such a ceremony, the 1957 Report wrote:

> We are convinced that all synodical action of this character should be approached and handled with a new and higher sense of its evangelical importance to a living Church. The Romans are right in making promulgation an event of joy and thanksgiving, and in proclaiming to the whole Church the life of a servant of God which has been grandly achieved. If a prescribed liturgical ceremony of that kind seems alien to ourselves, other ways of publication and celebration may appear.[17]

What is required is not a 'raising to the altars' in any technical way, but a joyful and eucharistic celebration whereby the additions to the calendar become more than the objects of synodical debate and examination. Every saint is different and so every inauguration of a new name in the calendar will call for a different emphasis and type of celebration, but it should not be beyond the ability of liturgists to devise something suitable wherever it is required.

The occasions on which such procedures will be used will be rare. With the initial reform of the calendar completed in 1979 and a list of new commemorations incorporated in the calendar, it will not be a frequent occurrence for a new name to be proposed. If it were to be agreed that the procedure should include a provision that a name must have been included in a diocesan calendar for, say, five years before it could be brought to the General Synod, the process would be slowed down considerably. There is no danger at all of the synodical procedures being 'snowed under' by proposals to add vast numbers of worthy Christians to the list of those to be commemorated.

A particular and unique opportunity was raised by the recent decision to include for the first time uncanonised Christian heroes in the calendar of the Church of England. In 1979, twenty individual Christians, ranging across the centuries from Julian of Norwich to Edward King of Lincoln, found a place in the English calendar. But the opportunity was lost when the Church of England failed to give consideration to the provision of a liturgical occasion in which these new names could have received recognition in an act of joy and thanksgiving.

In deciding who shall be included in new calendars, the Church of England may fear that, by abandoning the requirement for formal canonisation procedures, it will find itself accepting 'lower standards' of sanctity. The 1957 Report sounded a warning:

> The insertion of a name in the calendar as that of a holy man is not to be done lightly or without much consideration. There is no good basis in scripture, and for some centuries little in tradition, for the requirement that miracles must have been performed at the intercession of the person under examination, and any such requirement would certainly not be in keeping with the Anglican tradition and outlook. Nevertheless, we can learn much from that part of the Roman process which deals with the examination of the virtues. . . . There is a danger lest in the desire to fill a gap of three centuries in our calendars we add the names of people who were worthy rather than heroic, and so lower the idea of holiness to a more comfortable level.[18]

That is well said, though even a formal canonisation process has failed many times to prevent the inclusion of some men and women whose Christian virtue seems to have fallen short of heroism. Jerome is but one example.[19] The new English calendar includes on 26 September the commemoration of 'Lancelot Andrewes, Bishop of Winchester, 1626'. Andrewes was one of the more influential of the seventeenth-century Anglican divines who gave to the English Church that distinctive ethos that had lasted until the present reforming generation. His principal legacy to the Church has been in the field of spirituality through his *Preces Privatae*. His name was not included in the 1969 or 1976 proposals, perhaps because not all of his life seems to qualify as 'heroic'. The Revision Committee of the General Synod brought to the consideration of his name its usual hasty judgement. Three members had proposed his inclusion. The Committee recommended:

> Lancelot Andrewes has been added on account of his contribution to sacramental theology.[20]

In view of this it is profitable to examine what Andrewes' own sympathetic biographer, Paul Welsby, has to say about him:

> It is an old and inescapable dilemma which faces the historians—whether to judge a man by the accepted standards of his age or by his own ideals and religious profession. By contemporary standards Andrewes compared not unfavourably with his fellow bishops, but by his own declared profession the judgement must be less complimentary. To adapt the well known scriptural text, from one by whom much is professed of him is much expected. For this reason it is very doubtful how far Andrewes may be described as 'saintly'. A saint is one whose sanctity is not departmentalised but whose inner spiritual life is reflected in all he does and says. Hence a certain robust heroism is not seldom a characteristic of sanctity. The saint's daily life and intercourse is a reflection of the life of the Lord whom he worships and serves, and in that divine life while on earth were displayed an unshaken purpose, as unhesitating decisiveness, and a moral courage and integrity unto death. In so far as qualities can be discerned in the life of Andrewes in all its aspects, in that measure only can sanctity be ascribed to him. Perhaps his nearest title to sainthood is what is revealed in the *Preces*—that he knew himself to be a sinner.[21]

Welsby is hard on Lancelot Andrewes, though in that final sentence he reaches the heart of the matter. Andrewes is not the hero figure ten foot tall, so to speak, but he does seem to qualify for commemoration because he is still able to draw men and women nearer to God through his sanctity, the sanctity of the sinner revealed in the compelling prayer of the *Preces Privatae.* His inclusion in the calendar seems justifiable, but for that one reason alone, and not because of his contribution to sacramental theology. The Anglican authorities do not yet seem to be clear on their criteria.

Of course Andrewes' sacramental theology is not irrelevant to his case. Indeed it is the reason why he is suitable for inclusion where other less memorable men, just as pious, but not as learned and therefore lost in obscurity, are not. It is right that many theologians in the history of the Church from Justin Martyr to Dietrich Bonhoeffer should be considered for inclusion because reflection on their contribution to theological thought deepens the faith and understanding of the Church, provided always that the holiness of their lives or, at least, their desire to come closer to God is known and undisputed.

Some very strange criteria seems to have been employed in the selection of names for local calendars. That of the Diocese of Salisbury may be taken as a somewhat extreme example. Authorised in 1975 and 'gladly commended' by the bishop, it includes:

| | |
|---|---|
| 16 April | Benjamin JESTY, of Worth Matravers, pioneer in small-pox innoculation, 1816 |
| 21 May | Sir John THYNNE, of Longbridge Deverill, Founder of Longleat, 1580 |
| 19 Dec. | Joseph M. W. TURNER, Painter of Salisbury Cathedral, 1851 |

Many other worthy poets, artists, philanthropists, and scientists are in the Salisbury list. Sanctity, in the sense in which we sought to find it in Lancelot Andrewes, does not seem to have been a consideration. Jesty, with his very special contribution to medical knowledge and progress, was obviously a worthy man and a man through whom God worked. It seems right that the Church should thank God for him and use a commemoration of him to pray for all those involved in medical research. Nevertheless it does not seem right to list him as a 'hero of the faith' (to be fair to the Diocese of Salisbury, it does not use that term) and in referring the calendar to diocesan committees the Liturgical Commission were quite clear that they were asking local churches to consider the commemoration of men *of God.* As for Sir John Thynne's inclusion, if his only contribution was to found a stately home, it may be wondered whether the Diocese of Salisbury is not simply providing a list of interesting local historical personalities. Such a list is not without value, but its confusion with a list of the heroes of the faith is unfortunate. The saint must be seen to point to God. He or she may well point in that direction through art or through science. But there must have been in the life of the saint a conscious realisation that it was God that mattered in the end and God's grace that brought about new discovery or creativity.

The 1959 report also raised another question about procedure, this time concerned with where the pressure for the inclusion of a name should begin. Our examination of the cult of the saints in the first millennium bore witness to the fact that recognition came first in a local community and spread out from that. It was not imposed, at least initially, from above. As the 1959 report expressed it:

> A calendar of saints should proceed from the life of the Church rather than from the researches of an historian. It is true that the saints have an educative value and that a calendar may give a conspectus of the life of the Church throughout the centuries, but it is more important that the names in it should live in the devotion of the people, exciting them daily to the service of the Lord of the saints.[22]

There is much truth in that, though possibly too little distinction is drawn between the veneration of a saint, which is the spontaneous activity of the community, and the calendar, which is the responsibility of the ecclesiastical authority and in which balance, educative value, and other considerations have a place. In the long term the policy of allowing recognition to spring up locally is right and proper. But in our own day this is simply not possible. For four hundred years Anglicanism has on the whole not seen such spontaneous acclamation as part of its life. Even today communities of Christians will not see it as an exercise in which they can take part to name and celebrate new 'saints' of God. It will take a generation or two, perhaps more, before such a procedure becomes a natural part of the life of the Church at a local level. But in any case in the sort of 'global village' in which we live, the local cult in the isolated community will never be possible in the way it was a thousand years ago. The fact is that in a world of newspapers and television we are as likely to be moved to new Christian commitment by a Martin Luther-King as by some local saintly Christian worker, and as likely to come closer to God through reading and hearing about Thomas Merton as by a saintly parish priest. In the case at least of Luther-King the process by which he might be named in the calendar will not begin in his own community—such activities are not part of the tradition of the southern Baptist churches. For the time being it is the central church authorities that must take the initiative, sensitive always of course to the men and women in the local churches and what sort of Christian witness will move and inspire them, until the concept of recognition in our own day of heroic sanctity takes such a hold upon the Church that local initiatives begin.

We have noted two difficulties in the production of local

calendars—the use of false criteria producing historical rather than liturgical lists, and the reluctance in the local church after centuries of inactivity to take up the task of giving recognition to saints. Despite this, it is very desirable that the Church should give every encouragement to local communities to take up this challenge. Each diocese should devise its own calendar to supplement the national calendar and this should be approved in the Diocesan Synod and inaugurated by the bishop in some sort of liturgical ceremony. Diocesan commemoration will not, however, meet the need in many cases, for the names that are likely to mean most in a parish church are names of those associated with the life of the particular parish church and schools and institutions within it. If every man and woman whom any parish wished to remember were to be included in a diocesan calendar, the list would have more names than days of the year and, even though the observance of names in the calendar would be optional, still it would be an over large and impractical document. To use the Salisbury document again (because for all its faults, it does more than any other attempt to produce a genuinely local calendar), it includes the following entries:

3 Feb. Henry MOULE, Spiritual and Social Leader, Vicar of Fordington, Dorchester, 1880

20 Sept. Sir Robert NAPIER, of Dorchester, Judge and Benefactor, 1615

Both Moule and Napier mean something to the people of Dorchester. There are buildings in the town erected by them and bearing their names and both would qualify on any reasonable set of criteria. Their local commemoration within the parish of Dorchester would, therefore, seem totally appropriate. But it is much to be doubted whether their commemoration in any other part of the diocese of Salisbury makes very much sense. Such names are probably best not placed in a diocesan calendar, but observed only in the parish or parishes where they have significance. What procedure should there be to ensure some control over such commemoration? Each Parochial Church Council should give approval to local additions to the calendar and should then submit the names to the diocesan bishop for his approval. In making their submission they should be able to give the bishop an assurance that they have given careful consideration to the names and measured them up against a set of agreed criteria. To enable this to happen, the General Synod should amplify the bald statement in the recent reforms, 'Diocesan, local or other commemorations may be added to these lists,'[23] to include a set of guidelines for diocesan or parochial use, dealing briefly with the sort of issues that we have been examining in terms of the suitability, or otherwise, of candidates, and including some indications of appropriate liturgical provision, e.g. specimen collects. The involvement of the local bishop, which is not implicit in the statement above, is desirable, in order to prevent the inclusion of highly unsuitable or suspicious candidates. Similar rules should presumably exist to govern the choice of patron saints for churches.

## iii

Most of the criteria for the compilation of a calendar today have already emerged. The revisers of 1928[24] had some valid points, though they were not radical enough in their reform. We have already discussed the need for a major shift away from formal canonisation and also from antiquity. How then are changes to be made that come realistically to terms with the pastness of the past? One solution that does not seem to have been seriously considered is the abandonment of one of Cranmer's first principles, that of the exaltation of the apostolic age at the expense of the succeeding Christian centuries by making only biblical saints *red-letter* feasts. All subsequent Anglican revisions have accepted Cranmer's principle. But, however unparalleled the New Testament may have been, the witness of the communion of saints to God's power is in every age.

The Roman Church in England is not quite so tied to the apostolic age. Among the saints whose days are given the status of 'feasts' are a number of later saints: St. David (1 March), St. Patrick (17 March), St. George (23 April), The Beatified Martyrs of England and Wales (4 May), St. Augustine of Canterbury (27 May), St. John Fisher and St. Thomas More (22 June), St. Lawrence (10 August), St. Gregory the Great (3 September), The Forty Martyrs of England and Wales (25 October), and St. Thomas Becket (29 December). None of these observances commemorates anybody beyond the sixteenth century and it is a list that is certainly in no way ecumenical. But it remains a pointer to the fact that to 'up-grade' post-apostolic saints would not be an entirely new departure. The inclusion of the names of saints representative of the great doctors, mystics, and missionaries of the Church, and of national saints, and even perhaps the inclusion of modern figures of heroic sanctity, among the *red-letter* commemorations of the Anglican calendar would bring to it a new breadth in bold witness to the fact that sanctity is not trapped in the first century.

To turn to the lesser holy days: In view of all that has been said about the *pastness* of the past, there is an unanswerable argument for the inclusion of a good many Christian heroes of the last few generations, men and women whose *pastness* does not strike us so strongly. We have already noted that both the patristic age and the pre-conquest Church in England venerated Christians who had only just died. Today, however, there are those who argue that no man or woman should be canonised for fifty years after their death. If, for a moment, we accept that rule and apply it to the latest Anglican calendar, we find among saints of the last hundred years who died more than fifty years ago only three: James Hannington (1885), Josephine Butler (1907), and Edward King (1910). There would have been no shortage of other candidates among the following: George Selwyn (1878), John Bosco (1888), Bernard Mizeki (1896), Teresa of Lisieux (1897), Brooke Foss Westcott (1901), Charles de Foucauld (1916), Stewart Headlam (1923), Frank Weston (1924), and Frederick von Hugel (1925). Florence Nightingale (1910) was in the 1976 proposals, but struck out by 11 votes to 1 in the Revision Committee.[25] The omission of all these names, so that the last hundred years is represented only by Hannington, Butler, and King is very unimaginative.

The list above includes no names or heroic figures who have died in the last fifty years. But, quite apart from having no support in traditional practice, this is an unfortunate rule. The words of the 1969 report are a little ambiguous on this matter:

> In the compilation of a diocesan calendar, a diocese is not of course restricted to local saints; where they are concerned, it might be well to adopt the principle of the Protestant Episcopal Church in the U.S.A. that a person's name should not be added to the calendar until fifty years after his death, as a safeguard against the fancy of the passing moment. But we hope that where there is a popular demand or a local reason for the inclusion of any name in the calendar—whether a new name or an old one, whether local or already canonised or not—this will be recognised in the first place by the diocese, and the name taken into diocesan calendars.[26]

The Commission seems to be arguing for a fifty year rule in the case of local worthies, and even then it does not seem to want to make of it a hard and fast rule. Nevertheless the Revision Committee in 1977 interpreted the matter in a different way. Asked to consider the inclusion of Archbishop Temple and Archbishop Luwum, it replied,

> We were prevented from considering William Temple and Janani Luwum, although sympathetic to these proposals, for the reason that their inclusion would have breached the principle laid down by the Liturgical Commission that the calendar should not contain the name of anyone who has died within the last fifty years. We endorse this principle.[27]

But it is not a sound principle. Though the fifty year rule certainly safeguards the passing fancy, it all but ensures that when a person is finally observed changes in the conditions of life mean that he is already an archaic and distant figure. Only the cause of making the saints remote, of emphasising their *pastness*, is served by such a rule. Is there any reason why Geoffrey Studdert Kennedy (1929), Charles Gore (1932), Dick Sheppard (1937), Evelyn Underhill (1941), William Temple (1944), Pierre Teilhard de Chardin (1955), George Bell (1958), Pope John XXIII (1963), Albert Schweitzer (1965), Martin Luther-King (1968), Thomas Merton (1968), and Janani Luwum (1977) should not be considered? Though the sanctity of men like William Temple and Dietrich Bonhoeffer will not diminish, their relevance to present day Christians must inevitably diminish as the years go on. We should seek for them, not recognition for ever, but only for our own generations for whom they can be heroic and relevant figures. This century has been one as rich in diverse Christian witness as any other time. All these men and women had blemishes, but who can doubt that in the lives of all of them was the faith and integrity of those on their way to God? As witnesses to the possibility of living close to God in the conditions of the twentieth century they are powerful symbols of hope. Only formalised and long-drawn-out procedures could prevent their recognition in the calendar for so long that their relevance will have faded for us.

Revision of the calendar means major shifts of emphasis, not only away from canonisation and antiquity, but also from rigid orthodoxy and over-suspicion of other Christian communions.[28] Indeed the inclusion in the calendar of the great heroic figures of other Christian communions can make a wise and constructive contribution to ecumenical understanding, both in teaching us something about the founders and leaders of other churches and in providing suitable occasions on which to pray for these other churches. Any twentieth-century calendar should be *catholic* in the best sense of that word. It should reflect the life and witness of the Church in every land in every age. It should witness to every variety of sanctity—to the sanctity of priests and of lay-people, of those withdrawn from the world and of those in the midst of the world's bustle, of heroic and public lives and deaths and of quiet secret devotion, of Catholics and of Protestants. It should represent powerfully and compellingly the glorious heritage into which we have entered.

Such a calendar should have within it a considerable element of *choice*. It is better to produce a calendar with a great number of optional names, than a far smaller one in which it is expected that all the names will be commemorated. Although every diocese, parish, and institution should be able to supplement the list, the national calendar aims to provide a basic list suitable, through the exercising of options, for use in parish churches of every kind, cathedrals, schools, hospitals, theological colleges, religious communities, and a host of other institutions. It is right that places of theological learning should have the opportunity to commemorate in January Basil of Caesarea, Gregory of Nazianzius, Hilary of Poitiers, Charles Gore, Francis de Sales, Frederick von Hugel, and Thomas Aquinas, since all these men in their very different ways contributed significantly to the Christian understanding of faith in God. Equally it seems unlikely that the observance of all those days will be helpful or appropriate in most parish churches or in hospital chapels. The element of choice has always been present in Anglican observance. Indeed no *black-letter* observance is ever ordered. Nevertheless custom has usually been to keep all or no such days. In any future revision the priest's prerogative to choose should be clearly spelt out and the optional nature of commemorations underlined.

That said, it is equally desirable that whatever selection is made by the priest should still represent the catholic nature of the communion of saints. Under the present Anglican rules, for instance, it would be possible to commemorate every pre-Reformation saint, but to omit every Christian hero in the centuries since. This would give a very lop-sided picture of the communion of saints. Equally wrong would be a selection that included all Evangelical Protestant figures of the last few centuries, but omitted all Catholic ones. Some guidelines need to be given on selection, without imposing any too rigid solution.

A good deal has been said, and rather more implied, about the concept of *representation.* It was the principle on which the revisers of 1928 worked.[29] Subsequent revisers have not been so enthusiastic about it. The 1969 Report stated of its recommended names:

> (They) are all well known to people with a modest knowledge of the church's history. In general they are individuals whose life and history are well attested and of whose sanctity there is no doubt. They are not to be regarded as mere representative figures, chosen to represent a geographical area, a period of the Church's history, or to reflect some aspect of its life; they are individual men and women whose lives have excited others to sanctity.[30]

This may seem to be an argument against a *catholic* calendar of the sort we have advocated. But the Commission's view is not at odds with a representational approach. The Commission's insistence that there should be 'no mere representative figure' is right. Every name should be that of a compelling saint 'whose life has excited others to sanctity'. But there are many more such saints than could conveniently be placed in the calendar. The choice of which, among all the outstanding heroes of the faith, should be included must be made by a representational approach. Who can doubt, for instance, that there are a dozen outstanding saintly figures among the leaders of the eighteenth and nineteenth-century Evangelical revival in the Church of England? Henry and John Venn, for instance, would qualify. But one representative figure of that movement is probably sufficient, and Charles Simeon as suitable as any. What the commission was presumably warning against was an approach that said, for instance, that the Scandinavian Church must be represented and then proceeded to search for a suitable figure until it found the obscure Anskar, Bishop of Hamburg and apostle of Sweden, as the 1928 revisers did. Both heroic sanctity and representational usefulness are suitable criteria for inclusion, but the first must precede the second.

In order to appeal and make an impact the saint named in the calendar needs to come alive in people's imaginations. This is obviously more possible where either his life is well documented or, failing that, some particular story about him is well known and popular. Where neither exists it is very difficult to envisage the saint and to respond to what he stands for. For this reason there is very limited value in the 'group commemorations' in the New Anglican calendar. These are days under such titles as 'Saints and Martyrs of Australia and the Pacific'. The title is sufficiently abstract to leave the mind blank. Unlike the naming of a particular individual, it does not allow the mind to picture anything very helpful. The date chosen for the Australian saints (20 September) is the date of the martyrdom of Bishop John Coleridge Patteson. The Commission would have done much better to name him and, if necessary, add 'and all the saints and martyrs of Australia and the Pacific' than to give the day this rather anonymous and unimaginative title.

The final criteria for inclusion in the calendar must be historicity. Concern for truth must dictate the omission of the likes of Margaret of Antioch and Katherine of Alexandria. Saints who did not exist cannot be retained however many churches are named after them. The Church is made a laughing stock by such practice. There are a number of 'borderline' cases, such as St. George and St. Nicholas, whose existence is probably not much doubted but about whom next to nothing is known, to the extent that no year can be assigned to them. Saints in this category are probably best omitted from the calendar, unless there is a special reason for their retention. In the case of St. George, the fact that he is patron saint of England provides just such a special reason. St. Cecilia's Day is a problem, for there is no real evidence that any such saint ever existed, yet the day has special significance for church musicians. One possibility is to name it in the calendar 'Cecilia Day' and provide it with propers relating to church music, but without reference to the mythical virgin martyr Cecilia.

It is now possible to proceed, using a clear set of criteria, with the examination in some detail of the new calendars and to suggest a number of improvements in order to ensure a balanced and intelligent celebration of the communion of the saints.

# 9 *Some New Proposals*

## i

The most thorough going reform of the calendar in recent years has been that of the Roman Church. This came into effect on 1 January 1970. To commend its use the Pope issued an Apostolic letter on 14 February 1969:

> With the passage of centuries, the faithful have become accustomed to so many special religious devotions that the principal mysteries of the redemption have lost their proper place. This was due partly to the increased number of vigils, holy days and octaves . . . The purpose of the restoration of the liturgical year and the revision of its norms is to allow the Faithful, through their faith, hope, and love, to share more deeply in 'the whole mystery of Christ as it unfolds throughout the year.'
>
> In the light of this we do not feel that it is incongruous to emphasise also the feasts of the Blessed Virgin Mary, 'who is joined by an inseparable bond to the saving work of her Son' and the memorials of the saints, which are rightly considered as 'the feasts of our leaders, confessors, and victors'. 'The feasts of the saints proclaim the wonderful work of Christ in his servants, and offer fitting example for the faithful to follow.' The Catholic Church has always believed that the feasts of the saints proclaim and renew the paschal mystery of Christ.
>
> As the council properly pointed out, over the course of the centuries more feasts of the saints were introduced than necessary. 'Lest the feasts of the saints overshadow the feasts which recall the mysteries of redemption, many of these should be celebrated by local churches, countries or religious communities. Only those which commemorate saints of universal significance should be kept by the universal Church'.
>
> To put these decrees of the ecumenical council into effect, the names of some saints have been deleted from the general calendar, and permission was granted to restore the memorials and veneration of other saints in those areas with which they were traditionally associated. As a result, with the deletion of certain lesser known saints, saints born and raised in regions to which the Gospel was later

carried have been added. These representations of every group of people are given equal prominence in the lists of saints because they shed their blood for Christ or showed extraordinary signs of virtue.

Therefore a new general calendar has been prepared for use in the Latin rite which we feel is more in keeping with modern-day attitudes and approaches towards piety and which directs our attention to the universality of the Church. The calendar lists the names of remarkable persons who, each in his own way, offer the entire people of God outstanding examples of holiness which can greatly help Christians of every walk of life . . .[1]

Simplification has certainly been the main result of the revision. A great host of saints of doubtful historicity and little edificatory value have been swept away, leaving a calendar that is far less cluttered. The radical nature of the revision may be seen by examination of the reform in 1969 of the calendar of 1960 for just the first three weeks of the year.

JANUARY

| | | |
|---|---|---|
| 1 | OCTAVE DAY OF CHRISTMAS . . . 1st class | Renamed SOLEMNITY OF MARY, MOTHER OF GOD . . . Solemnity |
| 2 | | SS. Basil the Great and Gregory Nazianzen moved from 14 June and 9 May |
| 5 | Commemoration of St. Telesphorus, Pope and Martyr (Died about 135, possibly martyred, nothing else known about him) | Removed |
| 6 | THE EPIPHANY OF OUR LORD . . . 1st class | Now designated 'Solemnity' |
| 7 | | St. Raymond of Penyafort (optional memorial) moved from 23 Jan |
| 11 | Commemoration of St. Hyginus, Pope and Martyr, (Died about 142, probably not a martyr) | Removed |
| 13 | COMMEMORATION OF BAPTISM OF OUR LORD JESUS CHRIST . . . 2nd class | Moved to Sunday after 6 January, now designated 'Feast'. St. Hilary (optional memorial) moved from 14 Jan |
| 14 | St. Hilary, Bp of Poitiers, Confessor and Doctor . . . 3rd class | Moved to 13 Jan |
| | Commemoration of St. Felix, Priest and Martyr (Priest of the third century, lived at Nola near Naples) | Removed |
| 15 | St. Paul, the First Hermit, Confessor . . . 3rd class (4th century hermit, sometimes called 'Paul of Thebes') | Removed |

| | | |
|---|---|---|
| | Commemoration of St. Maurus, Abbot (6th century, brought up by St. Benedict) | Removed |
| 16 | St. Marcellus I, Pope and Martyr . . . 3rd class (Died about 310, probably not a martyr) | Removed |
| 17 | St. Anthony, Abbot . . . 3rd class | Now designated 'Memorial' |
| 18 | Commemoration of St. Prisca, Virgin and Martyr (Nothing is known) | Removed |
| 19 | Commemoration of SS. Marius, Martha, Audifax and Abachum, Martyrs (Persians martyred at Rome, date unknown) | Removed |
| | Commemoration of St. Canute, King, Martyr (Danish King, assassinated in 1086) | Removed |
| 20 | SS. Fabian, Pope, and Sebastian, Martyrs . . . 3rd class | Observed separately as 'Optional Memorials' |
| 21 | St. Agnes, Virgin and Martyr . . . 3rd class | Now designated 'Memorial' |

Simplification therefore means not only a reduction in the number of saints commemorated (from 16 to 8 in the 21 days set out above) but also a less complicated system of dividing them into 'classes'. Days are of three types. 'Solemnities' are the most important holy days. They are given liturgical provision of the night before the feast, by a 'first vespers' and sometimes by a Vigil Mass. The saints whose days are observed as solemnities are The Blessed Virgin Mary (four times), St. Joseph, St. John Baptist, SS. Peter and Paul, and All Saints' Day itself. Most of the biblical figures and a number of other saints (normally of national importance) have their days designated 'Feasts'. Unlike solemnities, they have no provision for the previous evening. The third, and by far the largest grouping, is 'Memorials'. Some of these are optional and others, obligatory most of the time, lapse if, for instance, they come in Lent. The simplification of the system is much to be welcomed and, where optional memorials are omitted, the calendar becomes very straightforward. The calendar for early January, for instance, without optional memorials reads:

| | | |
|---|---|---|
| 1 | SOLEMNITY OF MARY, MOTHER OF GOD | Solemnity |
| 2 | SS. Basil the Great and Gregory Nazianzen, bishops and doctors of the Church | Memorial |
| 6 | THE EPIPHANY | Solemnity |
| 17 | St. Anthony, Abbot | Memorial |
| 21 | St. Agnes, Virgin and Martyr | Memorial |

The choice of saints within the calendar is a far more intelligent one than in its predecessor. It will have been noted that the saints named in the early weeks of the year in the old calendar are all obscure, little or nothing being known about most of them. The loss, for instance, of SS. Marius, Martha, Audifax, and Abachum from the calendar is welcome. Nevertheless the revision remains a very conservative one judged by most of the criteria we have advocated. The rejection of the claims of all non-Roman saints reiterates the suspicion of all other Christian communions. Perhaps this is not surprising. The time has probably not yet come when the Roman Catholic Church can give any formal recognition to schismatic heroes of the faith. But it is sad that on 3 June the calendar commemorates only the Roman Catholics among the martyrs of Uganda.[2] A number of Anglicans died too under the cruel chief Mwanga, and their association with their Roman brethren in the liturgy of the day would be a pleasing ecumenical move. The recent canonisation of the Forty Martyrs and the observance of their feast in the English Church on 25 October is understandable, but again an ecumenical gesture would have been appropriate.[3] The requirement of strict orthodoxy also continues, as does the requirement that formal canonisation must precede entry into the calendar, but again it would have been very surprising if the Church of Rome, for all the changes it has made since the Second Vatican Council, had changed its outlook on matters such as these so quickly.

On the test of historicity, the new calendar is fairly responsible. Leaving aside the historicity of some of the feast days of the Blessed Virgin Mary,[4] the calendar seems to contain only two saints whose historical existence is sufficiently doubtful to require their exclusion in the cause of truth. The first is Saint Agatha, an obligatory memorial on 5 February. The calendar is content to describe her as a virgin and martyr. Whether it is right even to make that assertion is doubtful. Donald Attwater has written of her:

> There was certainly a virgin martyr named Agatha at Catonia in Sicily, who was venerated from early times; but nothing more is known about her. Her worthless legend, of which there are many versions, tells us that she was a girl of noble family who was pursued by a man of consular rank, named Quintian. When she rejected him resolutely, he proceeded against her as a Christian. Having been handed over to a woman who tried in vain to corrupt her, Agatha was tortured in various ways, and we are told that at one point St.

Peter appeared in a vision and healed her hurts. But eventually she died from her sufferings.[5]

It is difficult, on the evidence of that description, to see why Agatha is given the status she is in the universal calendar. The case of St. Cecilia, also commemorated as an obligatory memorial, on 22 November is stranger still:

At some uncertain date a lady named Cecily founded a church in the Trastevere quarter of Rome; at her death her body was buried in a specially honoured place in the Cemetery of St. Callistus. No more is known of her. But by the year 545 she was called *Saint* Cecily and honoured as a martyr.[6]

These two examples aside, the calendar is reasonable, though the stories of Sebastian (20 January), George (23 April), Pancras (12 May), Marcellinus and Peter (2 June), and Cosmas and Damian (26 September) are sufficiently obscure or legend-laden to suggest that they would have been better omitted. All of these are optional memorials.

But the principal interest lies in the question of antiquity. Has the new calendar been able to escape from the slavery of the past and include figures of more contemporary relevance? Biblical saints are well represented, as are other figures such as Anne and Joachim, the parents of Mary. Of the non-biblical saints who are named (and this excludes 'group commemorations' such as the Seven Holy Founders and the First Roman Martyrs), about 140 in all, 12 represent the third century, 21 the fourth century, 11 the thirteenth century, 22 the sixteenth century and 13 the seventeenth century. Almost inevitably the periods of the Fathers, the Medieval Church, and the Reformation and its repercussions are recognised more than any other. If only the obligatory memorials, and not the optional ones, are included, it is the fourth and eleventh centuries that predominate. Using the total calendar again, it is remarkable that every century is represented, though the tenth century can produce only Saint Wenceslaus (28 September), a duke of Bohemia of great piety, venerated, probably mistakenly, as a martyr.[7] Except in those centuries already mentioned, there is an average of four saints per century. The twentieth century cannot be expected to include many names, considering there are such complicated canonisation processes through which to go. In fact there are just two saints of this century. The first is the optional memorial of St. Maria Goretti, virgin and martyr, on 6 July. Attwater describes her claim to fame:

> When she was twelve she began to be pestered by the overtures of a young man, whom she repulsed. Eventually he attempted to ravish her, threatening to kill her if she resisted. Resist she did, and in a frenzy he stabbed her repeatedly with a knife, so that she died twenty-four hours later.[8]

Her dying words are said to have been: 'I forgive him for the love of Jesus, and I pray that he may come with me to paradise.' The other twentieth-century saint is St. Pius X on 21 August. A good and holy man, a true pastor, he was an illiberal pope, remembered above all for his attacks on 'modernism'. In their different ways, Maria Goretti and Pius are saintly figures. There was popular demand for the canonisation of both of them. But the particular Christian virtues to which they witness are not particularly compelling and it is sad that no saint has emerged to represent a sanctity in a world more like our own. Charles de Foucauld could meet such a need. He was a contemporary of both these saints.

An examination of the *representational* value of the new calendar reveals a strange balance. Two thirds of the non-biblical saints in it were born in Europe. One third of the non-biblical saints were born in Italy. A few belong to North Africa and the Middle East, a few to the historic churches of the East. Saints in some sense from the New or Third World are rare indeed—Paul Miki and his companions (sixteenth-century Japanese saints, 6 February), Charles Lwanga and his companions (the nineteenth-century Ugandan Martyrs, 3 June), Rose of Lima (sixteenth-century religious in Peru, 23 August) and Martin de Porres (seventeenth-century Peruvian 'black' saint, 3 November). Of course there are several saints of European origin who nevertheless gave their lives to work in colonies, including such outstanding men as St. Anthony Claret and St. Francis Xavier. Nevertheless it remains regrettable that the universal calendar is so dominated by Europe in general and Italy and Spain in particular.

The witness of holy women is also under-valued by the calendar. Only twenty-four non-biblical women are recognised. Sixteen of these are honoured in part at least for their virginity; fifteen of them were members of religious orders. Outstanding among these are Catherine of Siena (29 April) and Teresa of Avila (15 Oct) whose writings, in the fourteenth and sixteenth centuries respectively, earned them the title of 'doctor of the Church'. That recognition was a blow against the male domination not only of theology but of the calendar. Of the four women in the calendar who were not members of religious communities or virgins, Perpetua and Felicity (7 March) were martyred at Carthage in 203,[9] Monica (27 August) was the rather controversial mother of St. Augustine of Hippo, and Margaret of Scotland (16 November) was an eleventh-century queen and benefactor of the Church. The omission of any saint renowned simply for being a wise wife and mother is a loss.

Of the male saints, all but nine are clergy or religious. Again, the sanctity of the layman in the world has not been recognised. Those few who remained laymen are mainly kings and princes. It is a very priest-dominated calendar. St. Thomas More (22 June) stands out almost alone as representative of Christian faith lived out in ordinary life. Perhaps, among all the clerical saints, it is inevitable that he is a far more attractive and compelling figure.

Although there are some festivals of the Blessed Virgin Mary that have been removed from the new calendar, Our Lady continues to occupy a very full place in the calendar of the saints. Even if we exclude the Annunciation as being principally a feast of Our Lord,[10] we find no less than fourteen observances:

| | | |
|---|---|---|
| 1 Jan | SOLEMNITY OF MARY, MOTHER OF GOD | Solemnity |
| 11 Feb | *Our Lady of Lourdes* | *Optional Memorial* |
| 31 May | VISITATION | Feast |
| Sat after Pentecost 2 | *Immaculate Heart of Mary* | *Optional Memorial* |
| 16 July | *Our Lady of Mount Carmel* | *Optional Memorial* |
| 5 Aug | *Dedication of St. Mary Major* | *Optional Memorial* |
| 15 Aug | ASSUMPTION | Solemnity |
| 22 Aug | Queenship of Mary | Memorial |
| 8 Sep | BIRTH OF MARY | Feast |
| 15 Sep | Our Lady of Sorrows | Memorial |
| 24 Sep | Our Lady of Ransom | Memorial in England |
| 7 Oct | Our Lady of the Rosary | Memorial |
| 21 Nov | Presentation of Mary | Memorial |
| 8 Dec | IMMACULATE CONCEPTION | Solemnity |

The Solemnity of Mary on New Year's Day is an ancient feast, as its appearance in the earliest calendars show.[11] Our Lady of Lourdes recalls the appearance of the Immaculate Virgin Mary to Bernadette Soubirous in 1858. Our Lady of Mount Carmel owes its origin to the Crusades when Christian hermits established themselves in caves in the mountains: in the thirteenth century, they joined together in a religious community under the protection of the Blessed Virgin. Mount Carmel overlooks the plains of Galilee, not far from Nazareth. The Dedication of St. Mary Major commemorates the building of the oldest church in the western Church dedicated to Mary. It was erected in Rome by Pope Sixtus III after the Council of Ephesus in 431. Our Lady of Ransom is kept in England, our Lady being patron of the Church in England under this particular title. Our Lady of the Rosary has been celebrated since the Christian victory over the Turks at the Battle of Lepanto in 1571. The Presentation of Mary is a late medieval feast in the West (much earlier in the East) celebrating the alleged Presentation of Mary in the Temple at the age of three, an unlikely tale to be found in early apocryphal writings.

Fourteen feasts, of which only four are optional, seems excessive, and quite out of line with the general tone of the Council's decrees and the Apostolic letter. While the Roman Church retains its distinctive doctrinal view of the Assumption and the Conception, the celebration of these feasts is clearly right. The feast on 1 January has a long history behind it, though its disappearance for hundreds of years suggests it can be dispensed with and the Anglican solution of observing it as 'The Naming of Jesus' is probably happier.

The celebration of the Visitation has good biblical basis, of Our Lady of Sorrows a reasonable emotional appeal, and of the Birth of Mary a consistency with the celebration of the Birth of Our Lord and St. John Baptist. The value of the other observances is not so obvious. Five feasts of Our Lady seem adequate, even given the place that Roman Catholicism assigns to Mary. Certainly seven feasts in a little over sixty days (5 August–7 October) lacks sensibility to the fact that the observances must become routine, predictable, and 'stale' if they follow each other, on average, every nine days.

The new calendar transfers a number of observances to new dates. 'The General Norms of the Liturgical Year and The Calendar' lays down a number of sensible rules about the dates of observances:

> The Church has customarily celebrated the saints on their birthday, the day of their death. This also seems appropriate when proper celebrations are included in particular calendars . . . Celebrations for saints not included in the general calendar should be assigned to the day of their death. If the day of death is not known, the

> celebration should be assigned to another day associated with the saint, such as the day of ordination or the discovery or transfer of his body; otherwise it is celebrated on a day un-impeded by other celebrations in that particular calendar.[12]

Following these rules, the calendar has moved about forty per cent of the feast days. The usual reason is that a recent saint, the date of whose death is known, is now assigned that date in preference to a much earlier saint, the exact date of whose death is not known. Or else the removal from the calendar of an obscure saint has released a date, hitherto unavailable, for another saint. Sometimes the new date brings the Roman calendar in line with eastern practice. Sometimes the chief reason for a new date is to reduce the number of saints days in Lent and Advent. The alterations include three 'feast' days. St. Matthias is moved from 24 February out of Lent to 14 May. St. Thomas the Apostle is moved from 21 December out of Advent to 3 July. These are both welcome changes, though it is a pity that St. Thomas, a figure so associated with Easter, has not been moved to a date in Eastertide. The third translation is of the Visitation of the Blessed Virgin Mary from 2 July to 31 May. The approach has been relatively conservative. One might, for instance, have hoped to see St. Mary Magdalen brought into Eastertide, surely the right time for the First Witness of the Risen Lord, or St. Stephen moved to a date when, unlike 26 December, he is likely to be celebrated? But, on the whole, the moves are wise. Occasionally they will be unpopular. For instance, the traditional date for St. Alban, the first martyr in Britain, is 22 June. Rome logically says that because the actual date of Alban's death is unknown but the date of the execution of St. John Fisher is known to be 22 June, John Fisher is assigned to the 22nd and Alban moved. Those who have long observed St. Alban's Day on 22 June will object, but probably not for long. The new date will establish itself sufficiently quickly that soon nobody will remember the old one.

The General Roman calendar is only one part of the provision for commemorating saints in the Roman Church. As the 'General Norms' state:

> The general calendar includes the entire cycle of celebrations: the mystery of salvation as found in the temporal cycle and the saints, either those of universal significance which must be celebrated by everyone or others which show the continuity of holiness found everywhere in God's people. Particular calendars have proper

> celebrations arranged to harmonise with the general cycle. Individual churches or religious communities should honour in a special way those saints who are particularly associated with them. Particular calendars are to be drawn up by the competent authority and approved by the Apostolic See.[13]

The Diocesan calendar is the local norm, but entire provinces or national hierarchies may co-operate on a common calendar to ensure that the saints of a particular nation are commemorated. There is, for instance, a National Calendar for England. This is a particularly disappointing document. It raises to the level of a 'feast' several memorials in the general calendar, but the only new names it introduces are St. David (1 March), The Beatified Martyrs of England and Wales (4 May), St. Alban (20 June), Blessed Dominic of the Mother of God (26 August), our Lady of Ransom (24 September), St. Edward the Confessor (13 October), and The Forty Martyrs of England and Wales (25 October). It neglects most of the great British saints of the first millennium. The National Calendar for Wales is far more imaginative, naming Teilo, Bruno, Asaph, Deinoil, Winifrid, and many more. Sensible rules for the Diocesan Calendar are laid down:

> A diocesan calendar, in addition to celebrations of its patrons and the dedication of the cathedral, contains those saints and blessed who bear some special connection with that diocese, e.g. birth place, domicile over a long period, or place of death . . .
> When a diocese or religious community is favoured with many saints and blessed, the calendar of the entire diocese should not become disproportionately enlarged. Consequently:
>
> (*a*) There may be a common feast of all the saints and blessed of a given diocese or religious community, or of some category of saints;
> (*b*) Only the saints and blessed of special significance for an entire diocese or religious community may be honoured in the calendar with an individual celebration;
> (*c*) Other saints or blessed are to be celebrated only in those places with which they are most closely associated or where their bodies are buried.[14]

When these provisions are fully and imaginatively used, the diocese has the opportunity to enrich its commemoration of the heroes of the faith, and by venerating local heroes to bring the concept of the communion of the saints 'nearer home', so to speak. Where, however, scanty provision is made, the calendar in use will remain foreign, and specifically Mediterranean, dominated, and really very distant from local church history and devotion. As with the Anglican encouragement to experiment,[15] the response has not been overwhelming, though in the Roman Church local calendars and local initiative in framing them is not new.

ii

The story of Anglican Revision of the calendar in the twentieth century has almost been told. The proposals of 1928,[16] though not legal, were used in many churches because the provision of saints days was so much more sensible than that of the Prayer Book, though a number of churches used other calendars in various unauthorised missals. In particular the English Missal repeated, almost unaltered, the Roman calendar of the time. In 1957 the Archbishop of Canterbury's Commission produced its report, *The Commemoration of Saints and Heroes of the Faith in the Anglican Communion.* It examined in some detail the revision of the calendar in various provinces of the Anglican Communion outside the British Isles and suggested a way forward in England. In 1968 the Church of England Liturgical Commission issued a report entitled *The Calendar and Lessons for the Church's Year.* This issued a revised table of greater and lesser holy days, much in line with the 1928 proposals, but in addition provided for the first time in England a list of non-canonised heroes: 'Dioceses might like to consider the following list, which may serve as a stimulus to further discussion.'[17] The list also included post-Reformation Roman Catholic saints. Among the Anglican and Protestant selections were controversial ones such as George Fox (13 January), John and Charles Wesley (3 March), and John Bunyan (31 August). The names put forward for discussion were not debated in the General Synod and subsequent enquiries revealed that the invitations to the dioceses to consider local commemorations had met with very limited response. The commission therefore returned to the subject itself and in 1976 published *The Calendar, Lectionary and Rules to Order the Service* (GS 292). The proposals were similar, but not identical to, most of the previous report. The 'lesser Festivals and commemorations', as they were now called, were in two sections, Section A corresponding approximately to the 1928 proposals, Section B to the tentative list issued for discussion, though here a good many dates had been changed in line with Roman practice. After debate in Synod, the Report was examined and revised by the Revision Committee. A number of significant changes were made, though most of the more sweeping amendments were rejected. The division of lesser Festivals was abandoned and a number of the more controversial post-Reformation Protestant figures were omitted. The Revised text was issued as GS 292B in 1978 and authorised by the General Synod with few further alterations for use from October 1979.

The final calendar divides feast days into 'Principal Holy Days', 'Festivals and Greater Holy Days', and 'Lesser Festivals and Commemorations'. The Principal Holy Days are Easter Day, Ascension Day, Pentecost, Christmas Day, The Epiphany, Maundy Thursday, Good Friday, and every Sunday in the year. The Festivals and Greater Holy Days are the Patronal and Dedication Festivals of the Church, Ash Wednesday, the remaining days of Holy Week, the six weekdays of Easter Week, and twenty-six feasts of Our Lord, his Mother, and other biblical saints. These correspond to the Prayer Book *red-letter* days, save that two dates (St. Matthias and St. Thomas) have been changed and four feasts added—St. Mary Magdalen and the Transfiguration, which have featured in the calendar since 1928, and St. Joseph and the Blessed Virgin Mary, which are new. The lesser Festivals and commemorations are all optional. 'Diocesan, local, or other' commemorations may be added to them.

The revised calendar breaks new ground, at least in England, by its willingness to commemorate men and women who have not been canonised. Of seventy-three individuals outside New Testament times who are named, twenty-one have never been canonised. These include two pre-Reformation heroes, Julian of Norwich and John Wyclif. The others belong to the Reformation period or since, and all but two were Anglicans. The exceptions are William Tyndale, who really belonged to a much more thorough-going Protestantism and spent a good deal of time abroad with the continental reformers, and John Bunyan, a representative of English Protestantism. The calendar also recognises the claims of six Roman Catholic saints of the post-Reformation era—Francis de Sales, Thomas More, Vincent de Paul, Teresa of Avila, Francis Xavier, and John of the Cross. But it is less willing to recognise heroic sanctity in Protestant bodies.

In removing George Fox, the Revision Committee commented that

> We thought that the inclusion of George Fox despite his importance to English Church history would be inappropriate in an Anglican calendar.[18]

Isaac Watts was also removed. No explanation is given for this bias. It cannot be on grounds of orthodoxy, for Watts, for instance, was far more orthodox than Bunyan, who had no sacramental theology whatever. Indeed questions of right doctrine do not seem to have featured in the Commission's thinking, for the designation 'Teacher of the Faith' is used happily about Francis de Sales, John and Charles Wesley, and Richard Hooker, all of whom held rather different views.

In terms of historicity this must be judged a fine calendar. No saints are named whose existence is in real doubt. St. George is obscure, but in England the omission would be unthinkable. St. Nicholas is perhaps the strangest entry, though the Revision Committee made a good case for his inclusion:

> Nicholas of Myra, as the 450 churches dedicated to him witness, is widely venerated. As he is an important saint from the Eastern Church, to whom many churches are dedicated and after whom schools and hospitals are named, we felt him to be worthy of inclusion.[19]

But the real problems in terms of historicity have disappeared.

The calendar includes figures from every century save the ninth. The period of the fathers (3rd—4th century), the coming of Augustine and the spread of Christianity in both the north and south of England (the seventh century), the Reformation (the sixteenth century), and the time of Anglican individualism and consolidation (the seventeenth century) dominate, the seventh and seventeenth centuries both having as many as nine entries. The two millennia are almost equally represented, but commemorations tail off in the last one hundred and fifty years, which can produce only Edward King (1910), Josephine Butler (1907), John Keble (1866), William Wilberforce (1833), James Hannington (1885), and Charles Simeon (1836).

The balance of the calendar is not good. There are nine women and sixty-four men. There are fifty-five bishops, priests, and deacons. Not a single named saint was born in any of the 'new' countries, though some were there as missionaries. Sixty-three of the seventy-three were of European origin. Forty-one were

British, and, though it is right that a national calendar should reflect the life of the national church, this is probably too high a proportion. Learning and theological expertise counts for a good deal. A third of the entries are of theologians. Indeed learning counts for more than martyrdom in this calendar. The women are Agnes (virgin martyr), Perpetua (martyr), Catherine of Siena (mystic and teacher), Julian of Norwich (mystic), Clare (religious founder), Teresa of Avila (mystic and teacher), Hilda (abbess)—something of a stereotype of female sanctity emerges,[20] but Margaret (Queen of Scotland) and Josephine Butler (wife and mother, social reformer) restore the balance a little. Where the calendar is stronger than the Roman is in the provision of laymen. Charles I, George, Alban, Thomas More, Oswald, and Edmund are all martyrs. Charles, Oswald, Edward, and Edmund were kings. Thomas More, William Wilberforce, John Bunyan, and Josephine Butler were all people of striking individualism and appeal.

The omission of representatives of the newer churches is of course rectified in part by the provision of group commemorations, 'Saints and Martyrs of Africa', etc. The ineffectiveness of such festivals has already been pointed out.[21] But, accepting for one moment the criteria that many saints are included in group commemorations, that Protestants are suspect (an unexplained view), and saints of the last fifty years dangerous ( a view amply explained), there are still some obvious omissions, among whom must be—

| | |
|---|---|
| 10 Jan | William Laud, Archbishop of Canterbury, Martyr (1645) |
| 27 | Frederick von Hugel, Teacher and writer (1925) |
| 31 | John Bosco, Founder of the Salesians, Educationalist (1888) |
| 1 Apr | Frederick Denison Maurice, Priest, Teacher, Social Reformer (1862) |
| 3 | Richard, Bishop of Chichester (1253) |
| 12 Oct | Elizabeth Fry, Social Reformer (1845) |
| 27 | Alfred, King of the West Saxons (899) |
| 23 | Clement of Rome, Pope and Martyr (c100) |
| 1 Dec | Charles de Foucauld, Hermit, Spiritual writer (1916) |

The inclusion of a number of names like these would redress several imbalances.

The dates of the new Anglican calendar bring most of its

commemorations into line with the Roman Church. The exceptions are John Chrysostom (27 January instead of 13 September), Augustine of Canterbury (26 May instead of 27), Basil (14 May instead of 2 January), Alban (22 June instead of 20), Thomas More (6 July instead of 22 June), Dominic (4 August instead of 8), and Cyprian (13 September instead of 16). In the case of English saints, like Augustine and Alban, the unwillingness to move the commemoration is understandable.[22] In the case of foreign saints, and especially one like Dominic where incorporation into the Anglican calendar is new, it would be better to follow the rest of western Christendom. The new Anglican calendar is a remarkable improvement on its predecessors. There are a number of small changes that would enrich it further, and there are some more fundamental theological assumptions that need to be examined in relation to the commemoration of saints in Anglicanism. It is to be hoped that these are given consideration before a future revision.

## iii

Nearly every province of the Anglican Communion has been engaged in the revision of its liturgy in the last decade and new calendars have been authorised. It has already been noted that other provinces were ready to abandon old principles about antiquity, orthodoxy, and commemoration long before the Church of England came to consider the matter. It would not be profitable to examine each of these new calendars in turn, for they all follow either the modern Roman approach or the same sort of criteria as the latest English revision. It would be useful however to take just one foreign revision, the American one, because the Episcopal Church of the United States has approached its revision of the liturgy with great thoroughness, care, and scholarship, and taken a somewhat independent line. The American calendar authorised in 1976 in the new experimental Prayer Book includes 115 individual saints since New Testament times. Of these, fifteen are of the fourth century, seven of the sixteenth century, twenty of the nineteenth century, and six of the present century. The American Church, unlike both the Roman Church and the Church of England, places no great emphasis on the Reformation period. It does, however, lay great stress on modern centuries in a way that other calendars do not. Two thirds of the saints commemorated are European and nearly fifty are British, but the Church of the East is better represented than in most western calendars. The calendar makes no distinction between canonised and un-canonised figures and indeed includes a very high proportion of the un-canonised, about forty per cent. But every single one of these un-canonised post Reformation figures is Anglican or Episcopalian.[23] No non-episcopal Protestant hero has been included at all. Nor has any canonised saint of the post-Reformation Roman Catholic Church. Teresa of Avila, John of the Cross, Francis Xavier and others are all omitted. It is a thoroughly and exclusively Anglican document.

Its number of female saints is much the same as in other calendars—nine out of one hundred and fifteen. Its laymen are very few indeed—Bernard Mizeki, the African martyr; William Wilberforce; King Louis of France; and King Alfred of the West Saxons. Indeed the greatest criticism of all must be that, more than any other, it is a priest-dominated calendar, full of theologians and divines; and every single American saint of the last two hundred years is a priest or a bishop, without a layman or a laywoman anywhere, not even among the many missionaries who are named. It is, therefore, a strange calendar, strong where others are weak, yet in the end an unimaginative and rather narrow sort of document.

## iv

In the use of all modern calendars it needs to be emphasised again that choice must be exercised. The Roman calendar introduces an element of choice with its category of optional *memoria.* The new Anglican calendar makes all but the greater holy days optional, and even with these a variety of observance will be appropriate and this need not in all places include a celebration of the Eucharist. Yet a far richer provision for the observance of saints' days in the daily office, on something approaching the Roman lines, would enrich the worship at least of the clergy. Whoever has the responsibility for exercising the choices available must do so with sensitivity if the balance is to be maintained, if the catholic nature of the commemoration of the saints is to be seen.

There is little doubt that in the past the celebration of saints' days has obscured the development and celebration of the liturgical year. Saints' days have 'got in the way'. This should not be allowed to happen in the future and there is less excuse for it now that the liturgical year is more intelligently arranged. The exercising of choice should never mean a decision to celebrate so many saints' days that the liturgical season is obscured. Both the parish priest and those who make church legislation need to be aware of the *freedom* with which the commemoration of the saints is best accomplished. However carefully a calendar may be devised, however thoughtfully the claims to sanctity of a particular Christian hero may be examined, spontaneity must not be lost. The priest must celebrate and declare the witness of whatever Christian lives will edify his people and lead them into greater faith, and he must do it on the day that it is right to speak. He must not allow any calendar, however logical, balanced, and carefully devised, to enslave him. The saints were the greatest inspiration when the celebration of their glory was spontaneous. When too many rules took over they lost their appeal. Every priest could do much worse in drawing up the calendar for use in his parish than consult the people. 'What saints mean something to you?' 'What do you think a saint is?' 'What saints have you known?' That would be the beginning of a restoration of some spontaneity in the commemoration of the saints and of a return to the celebration of the saints as a dynamic activity of the Christian community.

It is probable that future revision of the calendar will be undertaken with a fair degree of ecumenical co-operation. This has certainly not been the case until now, and the new Anglican revision at some points shows itself to have failed to grasp the thinking behind the new Roman calendar, especially in the basic structure of the Sundays and seasons of the year. More radical changes should probably not be brought about without ecumenical good will, though that does not mean that the Church of England need fail to act on liturgical reform save to copy Roman innovations. A willingness to rethink the structure of the Christian year is needed if Anglican revision is to be more than a tampering with an out-dated cycle of celebrations.

How important in the life of the Christian Church is the commemoration of saints? For all the remoteness of some of them, for all the danger that they may obscure God himself and his son Jesus, some of them can still be sacramental signs of the divine love and power. People will learn of God and relate to him very often more through stories than through concepts. God is revealed in the stories of the saints and telling witness is given to his activity in human life. This witness is an affirmation that all the Christian people, living and departed, are one in the communion of saints. In that fellowship and solidarity lies the Church's confidence. For the God who acted in Jesus acted again and again in every age and acts now upon men and women who belong within the communion of saints no less than the Christian heroes of the distant past. But if the saints are at the heart of the Church's confidence, so too are they a sign of the judgement under which it lives. If God was able to do great things in the lives of these faithful ones of the past, how will his Church respond to the divine initiative today?

# *Notes*

*Chapter 1*

1. *Epistle of Barnabas* 4.12.
2. *The Shepherd of Hermas,* Similitudes 3; 4.1–3; Visions 1.3; 2.2; 7; 3.7; 4.3.
3. Justin, *Apology* 1.52; *Dialogue with Trypho* 40.
4. *Adversus omnes haereses* 5.31.1f.
5. *De anima* 55.8.
6. See pp. 8–10.
7. Ode 15.9–10.
8. Ode 42.15–17.
9. *Martyrdom of Saint Polycarp* 1.1.
10. IX.3.
11. XIV–XVII.
12. *Adversus omnes haereses* 3.1.
13. *The Passion of Saint Perpetua and Saint Felicity* V.
14. XII.
15. XXI.
16. *Martyrdom of Saint Polycarp* XIX.2.
17. Polycarp, *ad Philipp.* ix.2.
18. Clement of Alexandria, *Stromata* IV.vii.44.
19. Origen, *Selecta in Psalmos, hom.*III.1.
20. *Exhortations to Martyrdom* 3.9.
21. *To the Romans* iv.
22. *Scorpiace* VI.
23. John Chrysostom, *de s. Droside mart.* 2.
24. Similitude ix.5.
25. Vision III.5.
26. Matthew 27.51–53.
27. *Contra Celsum* viii.
28. *Martyrdom of Polycarp* XVIII; see pp. 4–6.
29. Augustine, *de cura pro motuis gerenda* 4.
30. *The Passion of Saint Perpetua and Saint Felicity* VII and VIII.
31. *De monogamia* 10; *de corona* 3.
32. *Ep.* 1.2
33. *De oratione* 14.
34. Hilary, *Liber de Synodis* 92; Basil, *Ep.* II.cciii.3; Gregory Naz., *Orat.* xxiv.19; xliii.82.
35. *Ep.* ccclx.
36. *Orat.*xxiv.19.

37. *Praepar. Evang.* XIII.11.
38. *In Act Apost.hom.* XXI.4.
39. W. Frere, *Studies in Early Roman Liturgy: I The Kalendar*, Alcuin Club collections No. XXVIII, 1930.
40. Hilary, *Contra Constantium* 8.
41. Frere did not draw up the information in this calendar in tabular form. But most of the information in it is from his book.
42. I think that 22 April in Frere's list on p. 98 of *The Kalendar* is a misprint. The paragraph that follows gives 14 April and so do all later commemorations.
43. Alexander, one of the seven brothers, is named in the canon.
44. See p. 17.
45. See p. 16.
46. John Chrysostom, *De Melitio Antiocheno* 3.
47. Sulpitius Severus, *Ep.* 2.
48. *Vita Ephraem Syri.*
49. *Vita s. Antoni* 93.
50. *Orat.* xxiv.11.
51. *Contra Vigilantium* 6.
52. *Contra Constantium* 8.

*Chapter 2*

1. See p. 12.
2. *De Civ. Dei* xxi.13, 24.
3. See pp. 33–6.
4. Augustine, *Ep.* 185.iii.12.
5. Optatus, *Libri* VII.iii.4.
6. See E. W. Kemp, *Canonisation and Authority in the Western Church* (Oxford 1948), pp. 32f.
7. Ibid., pp. 33f.
8. British Museum Cotton MS. Nero A.ii, ff3–8b. Quoted in Francis Wormald, *English Kalendars before 1100*, Henry Bradshaw Society, 1933.
9. Kemp, p. 52.
10. Early English Text Society cxvi.
11. See p. 28.
12. Kemp, p. 34.
13. *Hist. Eccl.* III.iii.
14. See pp. 28f.

*Chapter 3*

1. See Benedicta Ward SLG (ed.), *The Prayers and Meditations of St. Anselm*, 1973.
2. See Clifton Wolters (ed.), *Revelations of Divine Love: Julian of Norwich*, 1966.
3. See Dorothy Sayers (ed.), *The Divine Comedy: Dante*, 1949.
4. Thomas Aquinas, *Summa Theologiae* 3a.lix.5.
5. 1 Peter 3.19–20, 4.6.
6. *Summa Theologiae* II$^{a}$.lxxxiii.4.i.

7. *Summa Theologiae* II$^{a}$.lxxxiii.11.
8. *Summa Theologiae*, Supplement lxxii.1.
9. *Summa Theologiae* II$^{a}$.lxxxiii.4.
10. Ward (ed.), p. 113.
11. See p. 35.
12. Ward (ed.), p. 133.
13. Ward (ed.), p. 109.
14. See *The Golden Legend* (many editions).
15. See Nevill Coghill (ed.), *The Canterbury Tales: Geoffrey Chaucer*, 1951.
16. Recounted in Keith Thomas, *Religion and the Decline of Magic* (1973), p. 29.
17. H. Walter (ed.), *Exposition and Notes: William Tyndale* (Cambridge 1848), p. 105.
18. Walter (ed.), p. 119.
19. Quotations from Wyclif's writings are from T. Lechler, *John Wycliffe and his English Precursors* (1904), which, unfortunately, gives no exact references.
20. John Wyclif, *Trialogus* iii c. 30.
21. See J. Gairdner, *Lollards and the Reformation in England*, Vol. I (1908), p. 157.
22. Migne, *Patrologia Latina* cc, col. 235.
23. *Patrologia Latina* cc, col. 900f.
24. Kemp, pp. 87f.
25. Quoted by Kemp, p. 119, from *Annales Monastici* i, p. 344.
26. Kemp, p. 124.

*Chapter 4*

1. John Calvin, 'Reply to Cardinal Sadolet', in J. K. S. Reid (ed.), *Calvin's Theological Treatises* (Library of Christian Classics Vol. XXII, 1954), p. 239.
2. Calvin, *Institutes*, Book 3, Chapter V.
3. Matthew 5.26.
4. Calvin, *Institutes*, Book 3, Chapter V.
5. Ibid.
6. Calvin, *Institutes*, Book 3, Chapter XX.
7. Martin Luther, 'To the Christians in Riga', in T. G. Tappert (ed.), *Luther: Letters of Spiritual Counsel* (Library of Christian Classics Vol. XVIII, 1955), p. 197.
8. Ambrose, 'On Isaac or the Soul' viii 75, quoted in Calvin, *Institutes*, Book 3, Chapter XX.
9. Luther, 'To George Buchholzer', in Tappert (ed.), p. 306.
10. Calvin, *Institutes*, Book 3, Chapter XX.
11. Luther, 'To the Christians in the Netherlands', in Tappert (ed.), p. 193.
12. Hugh Latimer, 'Articles Untruly, Falsely, Uncharitably Imputed to me by Dr. Powell of Salisbury', in G. E. Corrie (ed.), *Sermons and Remains of Hugh Latimer* (Parker Society, Cambridge 1844), p. 236.
13. Thomas Cranmer, 'Answers to the Fifteen Articles of the Rebels', in J. E. Cox (ed.), *Miscellaneous Writings and Letters of Thomas Cranmer* (Parker Society, Cambridge 1844), p. 181.
14. Myles Coverdale, 'The Defence of a Certain Poor Christian Man', in G.

Pearson (ed.), *Remains of Myles Coverdale* (Parker Society, Cambridge 1844), pp. 472–474.

15. Coverdale, 'The Carrying of Christ's Cross', in Pearson (ed.), pp. 258f, 269ff.

16. John Hooper, 'A Declaration of Christ and his Office', in S. Carr (ed.), *Early Writings of John Hooper* (Parker Society, Cambridge 1843), pp. 34f.

17. Coverdale, 'The Carrying of Christ's Cross', in Pearson (ed.), p. 260.

18. Latimer, 'Sermon preached on the Fourth Sunday after Epiphany 1552', in Corrie (ed.), p. 186. See also p. 88.

19. Latimer, 'Articles Untruly, Falsely, Uncharitably Imputed to me by Dr. Powell of Salisbury', in Corrie (ed.), p. 234.

20. Hooper, 'A Declaration of Christ and his Office', in Carr (ed.), p. 36.

21. Latimer, 'A Sermon preached at Bexterly on Christmas Day 1552', in Corrie (ed.), p. 88.

22. John Jewel, 'The Reply to Harding's Answer', in J. Ayre (ed.), *The Works of John Jewel* (Parker Society, Cambridge 1845), pp. 644–68.

23. Nicholas Ridley, 'A Treatise of Dr. Nicholas Ridley concerning Images', in H. Christmas (ed.), *The Works of Nicholas Ridley* (Parker Society, Cambridge 1841), pp. 83–96.

24. Jewel, 'The Reply to Harding's Answer', in Ayre (ed.), p. 660.

25. Hooper, 'A Declaration of Christ and his Office', in Carr (ed.), p. 39.

26. Jewel, 'The Reply to Harding's Answer', in Ayre (ed.), p. 666.

27. Cranmer, 'Correction of the Institution of a Christian Man by Henry VIII with Archbishop Cranmer's Annotations', in Cox (ed.), p. 101.

28. Hooper, 'A Declaration of Christ and his Office', in Carr (ed.), p. 38.

29. See letters written by Thomas Cranmer in Cox (ed.), pp. 490, 510.

30. Latimer, 'Articles Untruly, Falsely, Uncharitably Imputed to me by Dr. Powell of Salisbury', in Corrie (ed.), p. 233.

31. Jewel 'The Reply to Harding's Answer', in Ayre (ed.), p. 668.

32. See letters written by Thomas Cranmer in Cox (ed.), pp. 490, 510.

33. Ridley, 'Injunctions of Nicholas Bishop of London', in Christmas (ed.), p. 320.

34. John Aubrey, *Gentilisme*, quoted in Keith Thomas, *Religion and the Decline of Magic*, p. 81.

35. See letter written by Thomas Cranmer in Cox (ed.), p. 510.

36. See C. Lloyd, *Formularies of Faith put forward by Authority during the Reign of Henry VIII* (Oxford 1825), pp. 14f.

37. *Conc. Trid. Sess. xxv, De invoc. vener, et reliq. sanctorum, et sac. imag.*, quoted in Darwell Stone, 'Invocation of Saints', *Church Quarterly Review*, January 1899.

38. 'The Supper of the Lord and the Holy Communion, commonly called the Mass', in the *Book of Common Prayer* of 1549.

39. 'The Lord's Supper or Holy Communion', in the *Book of Common Prayer* of 1552.

40. 'The Burial of the Dead', in the *Book of Common Prayer* of 1552.

41. For a fuller discussion see Darwell Stone, pp. 292–95.

42. See pp. 51–4.

43. See, for instance, G. J. Maclear and W. W. Williams, *An Introduction to the Articles of the Church of England* (1895), p. 263.

44. See J. Wickham Legg (ed.), *Cranmer's Liturgical Projects*, Henry Bradshaw Society, 1915.

45. Wormald (ed.), *English Kalendars before 1100*, p. 154.
46. See p. 20.
47. See Wickham Legg (ed.).
48. See J. Ketley (ed.), *The Two Liturgies*, Cambridge 1844.
49. But a solution is well argued by F. E. Warren in Vernon Staley (ed.), *Hierurgia Anglicana* Part III (1902), pp. 250–6.

## *Chapter 5*

1. W. Orme (ed.), *The Works of Richard Baxter*, 1830.
2. Thomas Morton, *A Catholic Appeal for Protestants*, quoted in Ian Ramsey (ed.), *Prayer and the Departed* (1971), p. 75.
3. William Wake, 'A Discourse on Purgatory', in *Enchiridion Theologicum Anti-Romanum* Vol. III (Oxford 1837), pp. 526–31.
4. *The Works of Joseph Hall*, Vol. 5 (Oxford 1837), p. 442.
5. William Nicholls, *A Comment on the Book of Common Prayer* (1710), additional notes, p. 64.
6. F. E. Brightman (ed.), *Preces Privatae* (1903), p. 273.
7. 'A Dissuasive from Popery', Part I, Chapter I, in R. Heber (ed.), *The Works of Jeremy Taylor*, Vol. X (1828), pp. 147–9.
8. 'The Answer to la Milletière', in *The Works of John Bramhall* (Oxford 1842), pp. 59f.
9. William Forbes, *Considerationes Modestae* (Oxford 1850), pp. 91f.
10. John Keble (ed.), *The Works of Richard Hooker*, Vol. 3 (7th ed., Oxford 1888), pp. 872f.
11. *The Works of John Bramhall*, pp. 57f.
12. *The Works of Joseph Hall*, Vol. 9, p. 368.
13. *Considerationes Modestae*, pp. 229–31.
14. R. Heber (ed.), Vol. X, pp. 223f.
15. 'Funeral Sermon for Lady Margaret Mainard', in W. Benham (ed.), *The Prose Works of Thomas Ken* (1889), p. 65.
16. 'Just Weights and Measures', in *The Works of Herbert Thorndike* (Oxford 1844), Vol. 5, p. 248.
17. 'An Epilogue to the Tragedy of the Church of England', Book III, in *The Works of Herbert Thorndike*, Vol. 4, Part ii, pp. 768–79.
18. Richard Montague, *Immediate Address unto God Alone* (1624), pp. 107–9.
19. *The Works of Joseph Hall*, Vol. 7, p. 262.
20. Edward Pusey, *Letter to R. W. Jelf* (Oxford 1841), pp. 79f.
21. Session 25.
22. Edward Pusey, *Eleven Addresses to the Companions of the Love of Jesus* (Oxford 1868), pp. 127–34.
23. 'Fellowship with the Saints', in R. F. Wilson (ed.), *Outlines of Instructions or Meditations by John Keble* (Oxford 1880), p. 291.
24. See p. 66.
25. 'The Saints' Nearness to Christ', in R. F. Wilson (ed.), p. 295.
26. Eric Kemp tells the story in *Canonisation and Authority in the Western Church*, pp. 134f.
27. See pp. 57–60.

28. *The Commemoration of Saints and Heroes in the Anglican Communion* (1957), pp. 31f.

29. Ibid, p. 43.

30. But search in vain for these in modern editions of *The Book of Common Prayer.* For by an act of 1859 the service for 30 January ceased to be printed in the Prayer Book, and the Queen's printers considered that the authority of the act extended to the removal of the name also from the calendar—probably rightly.

31. 'King Charles the Martyr', in *The Christian Year*, Oxford 1827.

32. See below, pp. 78–83.

33. For what Anglican provinces abroad have done, see below, pp. 156f.

*Chapter 6*

1. For an outline of them, see Geoffrey Cuming, *A History of Anglican Liturgy,* 1969.

2. 'Occasional Prayers and Thanksgivings: The Prayers', No. 32, second and third alternatives.

3. See p. 55.

4. In the order for 'The Burial of the Dead'; these are the words that give rise, from their Latin text, to talk of a *Requiem* mass.

5. In an order for 'Prime'.

6. 'Occasional Prayers and Thanksgivings: The Prayers', No. 32, first alternative.

7. See the next section below.

8. *The English Missal* (3rd ed., 1958), pp. 839, 843.

9. See p. 20.

10. Donald Attwater, *The Penguin Dictionary of Saints* (1965), pp. 73f.

11. Attwater, p. 228.

12. Attwater, pp. 209f; Attwater gives an account of a quite preposterous legend.

13. *The Commemoration of Saints and Heroes in the Anglican Communion*, pp. 33f.

14. See pp. 4–6.

15. See p. 28.

16. David Knowles in Maisie Ward (ed.), *The English Way*, 1933.

17. See p. 43.

*Chapter 7*

1. See Ian Ramsey (ed.), *Prayer and the Departed*, p. 14.

2. The tone of the Psalter is unmistakable, despite Ps. 139 ('If I go down to the grave, thou art there also').

3. The Old Testament views and the impossibility of building a theology upon them have been well set out in Paul Badham, *Christian Beliefs about Life after Death* (1976), pp. 31–7.

4. The development in New Testament thought is clearly set out by David Edwards, *The Last Things Now* (1969), pp. 47–53.

5. Emil Brunner, *Dogmatics*, Vol. III *The Christian Doctrine of the Church, Faith and the Consummation* (1962), p. 405.
6. Matthew 25.31–46.
7. 1 Corinthians 15, especially vv. 50ff.
8. Karl Rahner, *On the Theology of Death* (1965), p. 8.
9. Dennis Nineham, *The Use and Abuse of the Bible* (1976), pp. 253f.
10. See pp. 35f.
11. Ian Ramsey (ed.), *Prayer and the Departed*, pp. 47–66.
12. See Albert Schweitzer, *The Quest of the Historical Jesus* (1911), esp. p. 397.
13. Emil Brunner, *Eternal Hope* (1954), p. 98.
14. John Macquarrie, *Principles of Christian Theology* (1960), p. 325.
15. John Hick, *Death and Eternal Life* (1976), pp. 238f.
16. Hick, pp. 413–21. Paul Badham answers the arguments well in *Christian Beliefs about Life after Death*, pp. 65–84.
17. Paul Tillich, *Systematic Theology*, Vol. 3 (Chicago 1963), pp. 440f.
18. Michael Ramsey, *Introducing the Christian Faith* (1961), pp. 80f.
19. John Baillie, *And the Life Everlasting* (Oxford 1934), p. 249.
20. Hebrews 11.40.
21. Ian Ramsey (ed.), *Prayer and the Departed.*
22. Offertory for All Souls' Day in *The English Missal*, p. 843.
23. *The English Hymnal*, No. 351 (and many other service books).
24. *Alternative Services Series 3: Funeral Services* (1975), p. 37.
25. Ian Ramsey, *Our Understanding of Prayer* (1971), p. 22.
26. Ian Ramsey (ed.), *Prayer and the Departed*, pp. 17f.
27. Ibid, pp. 55, 59.
28. Opening Prayers for the first Mass of All Souls' Day in *The Roman Missal.*
29. See p. 87.
30. See pp. 95f.
31. Attwater, *The Penguin Dictionary of Saints*, p. 186.
32. See pp. 78–80.

*Chapter 8*

1. *The Calendar, Lectionary and Rules to Order the Service 1976*, A Report by the Liturgical Commission of the General Synod of the Church of England, GS 292.
2. Ibid, p. 5.
3. GS 292B, p. 23.
4. See below.
5. Matthew 16.13–end.
6. John 21.15–22.
7. GS 292B among them.
8. *The Calendar and Lessons for the Church's Year*, A Report of the Church of England Liturgical Commission (1969), p. 16.
9. 'St. Mary the Virgin, Mother of our Lord Jesus Christ'.
10. GS 292, p. 6.
11. See above, pp. 119f.

12. See above, pp. 96f.
13. See above, pp. 11–15.
14. See above, pp. 26–9.
15. *The Commemoration of Saints and Heroes in the Anglican Communion*, p. 35.
16. Unfortunately there is no public record of the Commission's deliberations on this or any other matter, but Commission members have admitted that the drawing up of a calendar was a relatively arbitrary matter and the records of the Synod Revision Committee indicate a less than thorough examination of matters raised with them.
17. *The Commemoration of Saints and Heroes in the Anglican Communion*, p. 72.
18. Ibid, pp. 66f.
19. See above, pp. 118–19.
20. GS 292X, p. 31.
21. Paul Welsby, *Lancelot Andrewes 1555–1626* (1958), p. 273.
22. *The Commemoration of Saints and Heroes in the Anglican Communion*, p. 67.
23. GS 292B, p. 8.
24. See above, pp. 83–9.
25. GS 292X, p. 27.
26. *The Calendar and Lessons for the Church's Year*, p. 15.
27. GS 292X, p. 31.
28. See above, pp. 115f.
29. See above, pp. 85f.
30. *The Calendar and Lessons for the Church's Year*, p. 14.

*Chapter 9*

1. Apostolic letter: *Approval of the General Norms for the liturgical year and the new General Roman Calendar*. The text is reproduced in full in *The Roman Missal*. The quotations within the Apostolic letter are from documents of the Second Vatican Council.
2. The Feast of St. Charles Lwanga and his companions, martyrs.
3. See below, p. 153.
4. See below, pp. 148f.
5. Attwater, *The Penguin Dictionary of Saints*, p. 34.
6. Ibid, p. 81.
7. Other saints, such as Romuald, Henry, and Stephen of Hungary were born in the 10th century, but they were at their most influential in the 11th century.
8. Attwater, p. 236.
9. See above, pp. 6f.
10. See above, pp. 122–4.
11. See above, p. 23.
12. To be found, among other places, in *The St. Luke's Daily Missal*, p. xciii.
13. Ibid, p. xci.
14. Ibid, p. xcii.
15. See above, pp. 133–6.
16. See above, pp. 83–9.
17. Page 15.

18. GS 292X, p. 27.
19. Ibid, p. 31.
20. In all these calendars I have regarded Anne, the mother of the Blessed Virgin Mary, as belonging to the New Testament period, though of course she is not mentioned in the canonical scriptures.
21. See above, p. 141.
22. But see above, p. 150.
23. The American Church, with some logic, regards William Tyndale as 'Anglican', but see above, p. 153.

# *Select Bibliography*

(The place of publication of books is London unless otherwise stated.)


ATTWATER, D., *The Penguin Dictionary of Saints*, 1965.
AYRE, J. (ed.), *The Works of John Jewel*, Parker Society, Cambridge 1845.
BADHAM, P., *Christian Beliefs about Life after Death*, 1976.
BAILLIE, J., *And The Life Everlasting*, Oxford 1934.
BENHAM, W. (ed.), *The Prose Works of Thomas Ken*, 1889.
BOROS, L., *The Moment of Truth*, 1965.
BRANDON, S. G. F., *The Judgement of the Dead*, 1967.
BRIGHTMAN, F. E. (ed.), *Preces Private of Lancelot Andrewes*, 1903.
BRUNNER, E., *Dogmatics*, Vol. III *The Christian Doctrine of the Church, Faith and the Consummation*, 1962.
BRUNNER, E., *Eternal Hope*, 1954.
CAIRD, G. B. *et al*, *The Christian Hope*, 1970.
CARR, S. (ed.), *Early Writings of John Hooper*, Parker Society, Cambridge 1843.
CHRISTMAS, H. (ed.), *The Works of Nicholas Ridley*, Parker Society, Cambridge 1841.
COGHILL, N. (ed.), *The Canterbury Tales: Geoffrey Chaucer*, 1951. *Commemoration of Saints and Heroes in the Anglican Communion, The*, 1957.
CORRIE, G. E. (ed.), *Sermons and Remains of Hugh Latimer*, Parker Society, Cambridge 1844.
COX, J. E. (ed.), *Miscellaneous Writings and Letters of Thomas Cranmer*, Parker Society, Cambridge 1844.
CUMING, G., *A History of Anglican Liturgy*, 1969.
EDWARDS, D., *The Last Things Now*, 1969.
FARMER, D. H., *The Oxford Dictionary of Saints*, Oxford 1978.
FARRER, A., *The End of Man*, 1973.
FORBES, W., *Considerationes Modestae*, Oxford 1850.
FRERE, W., *Studies in Early Roman Liturgy: I The Kalendar*, Alcuin Club Collections No. XXVIII, 1930.
GAIRDNER, J., *Lollards and the Reformation in England*, Vol. I, 1908.
HEBER, R. (ed.), *The Works of Jeremy Taylor*, Vol. X, 1828.
HICK, J., *Death and Eternal Life*, 1976.
KEBLE, J., *The Christian Year*, Oxford 1827.
KEBLE, J. (ed.), *The Works of Richard Hooker*, Vol. 3 (7th ed.), Oxford 1888.
KEMP, E. W., *Canonisation and Authority in the Western Church*, Oxford 1948.
KETLEY, J. (ed.), *The Two Liturgies*, Parker Society, Cambridge 1844.
LECHLER, J., *John Wycliffe and his English Precursors*, 1904.
LEGG, J. Wickham (ed.), *Cranmer's Liturgical Projects*, Henry Bradshaw Society, 1915.

LLOYD, C., *Formularies of Faith put forward by Authority during the Reign of Henry VIII*, Oxford 1825.
MACLEAR, G. J. and WILLIAMS, W. W., *An Introduction to the Articles of the Church of England*, 1895.
MACQUARRIE, J., *Principles of Christian Theology*, 1960.
MONTAGUE, R., *Immediate Address unto God Alone*, 1624.
NICHOLLS, W., *A Comment on the Book of Common Prayer*, 1710.
NINEHAM, D. E., *The Use and Abuse of the Bible*, 1976.
ORME, W. (ed.), *The Works of Richard Baxter*, 1830.
PATERNOSTER, M., *Thou art there also*, 1967.
PEARSON, G. (ed.), *Remains of Myles Coverdale*, Parker Society, Cambridge 1844.
PITTENGER, N., *'The Last Things' in a Process Perspective*, 1970.
PUSEY, E. B., *Eleven Addresses to the Companions of the Love of Jesus*, Oxford 1868.
PUSEY, E. B., *Letter to R. W. Jelf*, Oxford 1841.
RAHNER, K., *On the Theology of Death*, 1965.
RAMSEY, I., *Our Understanding of Prayer*, 1971.
RAMSEY, I. (ed.), *Prayer and the Departed*, 1971.
RAMSEY, A. M., *Introducing the Christian Faith*, (1961).
REID, J. K. S. (ed.), *Calvin's Theological Treatises*, Library of Christian Classics, Vol. XXII, 1954.
ROBINSON, J. A. T., *In the End, God*, 1950.
SATGE, J. de, *Christ and the Human Prospect*, 1978.
SAYERS, D. (ed.), *The Divine Comedy: Dante*, 1949.
SCHWEITZER, A., *The Quest of the Historical Jesus*, 1911.
STALEY, V. (ed.), *Hierurgia Anglicana*, Part III, 1902.
STONE, D., 'Invocation of Saints', *Church Quarterly Review*, January 1899.
TAPPERT, T. G. (ed.), *Luther: Letters of Spiritual Counsel*, Library of Christian Classics, Vol. XVIII, 1955.
THOMAS, K., *Religion and the Decline of Magic*, 1973.
TILLICH, P., *Systematic Theology*, Vol. 3, Chicago 1963.
WAKE, W., *Enchiridion Theologicum anti-Romanum*, Vol. III, Oxford 1837.
WALTER, H. (ed.), *Exposition and Notes: William Tyndale*, Cambridge 1848.
WARD, B. (ed.), *The Prayers and Meditations of Saint Anselm*, 1973.
WARD, M., *The English Way*, 1933.
WELSBY, P., *Lancelot Andrews 1558–1626*, 1958.
WILES, M., *The Remaking of Christian Doctrine*, 1973.
WILSON, R. F. (ed.), *Outlines of Instructions or Meditations by John Keble*, Oxford 1880.
WOLTERS, C. (ed.), *Revelations of Divine Love: Julian of Norwich*, 1966.
*Works of Herbert Thorndike, The*, Oxford 1844.
*Works of John Bramhall, The*, Oxford 1842.
*Works of Joseph Hall, The*, Oxford 1837.

# *Index of Names*

# Index of Subjects